nassp®
leading schools

Breaking Ranks®

The Comprehensive Framework for School Improvement

FOR K–12 SCHOOL LEADERS

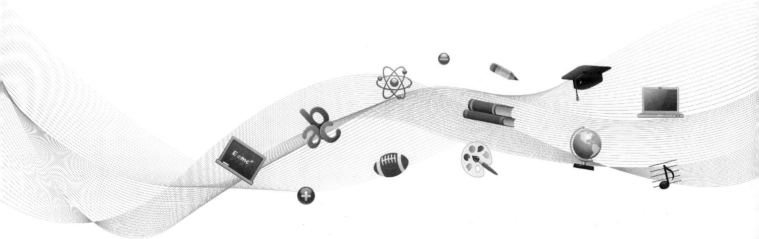

1904 Association Drive
Reston, VA 20191-1537
nassp@nassp.org
www.nassp.org

ISBN 978-0-88210-384-6

Contents

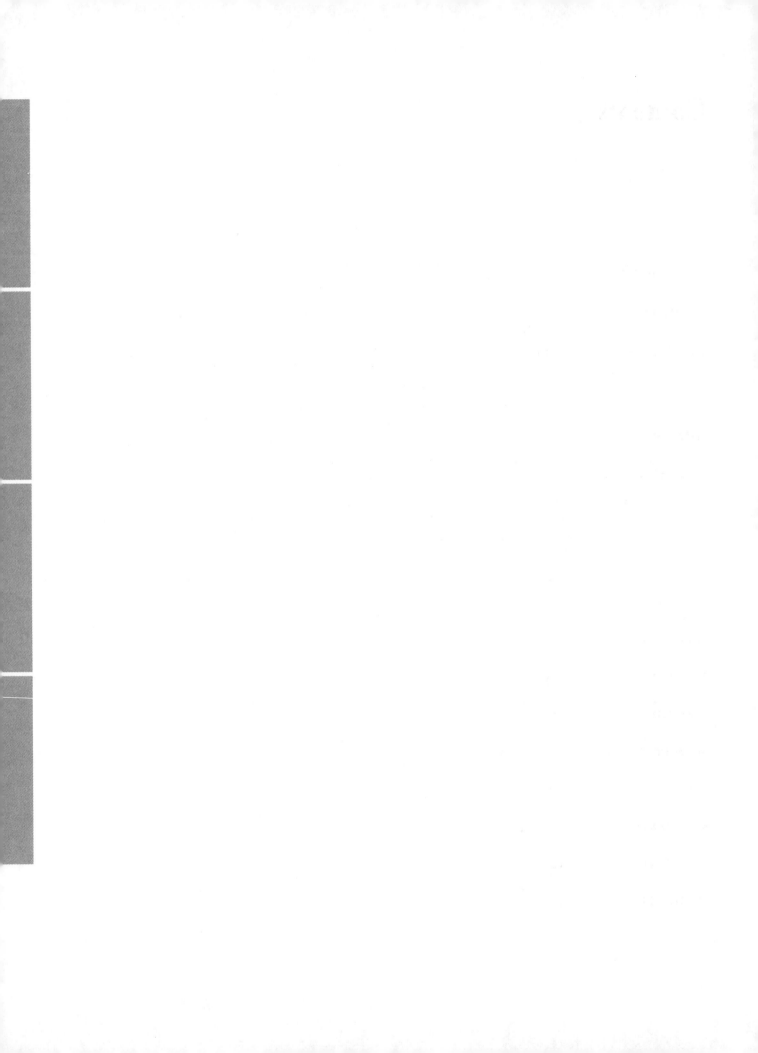

In Memory

John A. Lammel

Breaking Ranks: The Comprehensive Framework for School Improvement rests upon the foundation of the original *Breaking Ranks: Changing an American Institution* (1996). John A. Lammel, NASSP president from 1990 to 1991 and NASSP director of high school services from 1993 until 2000, was instrumental in guiding the development of the original *Breaking Ranks* publication and led the dissemination and advocacy for that groundbreaking school reform publication. With his leadership, the 1996 *Breaking Ranks* publication became a major factor in improving high schools across the United States and internationally.

We are saddened by the passing of John Lammel on January 14, 2011, but are honored to memorialize his important contribution to the foundation of this latest publication and to acknowledge his memory, history, and legacy with the *Breaking Ranks* publications.

Dedication

Breaking Ranks: The Comprehensive Framework for School Improvement is dedicated to Gerald N. Tirozzi, NASSP executive director from 1999 to June 30, 2011. His support and advocacy for the *Breaking Ranks* series is a major factor in the release of this publication. During his career, Tirozzi has been an active champion for improved schools. His recurring message at the local, state, and national levels is about providing increased learning opportunities for every child. He saw *Breaking Ranks* as a channel to carry his vision about school improvement to the nation. Beginning with the release of *Breaking Ranks II: Strategies for Leading High School Reform* (2004) and moving through *Breaking Ranks in the Middle: Strategies for Leading Middle Level Reform* (2006), *Breaking Ranks: A Field Guide for Leading Change* (2009), *10 Skills for Successful School Leaders* (2010), and the current book, *Breaking Ranks: The Comprehensive Framework for School Improvement* (2011), the *Breaking Ranks* series now totals five definitive publications that address the "what," "how," and "who" of school improvement. This publication represents the manifestation of Tirozzi's vision.

Acknowledgements

NASSP would like to thank the following people and organizations for their contributions to this book:

- NASSP staff members Karen Danto, Dick Flanary, Josephine Franklin, Carolyn Glascock, Patti Kinney, Anne Knudsen, John Nori, Peter Reed, Judy Richardson, Mel Riddile, and Lisa Schnabel.

- Practitioners at the elementary, middle level, high school, and university levels who read drafts, wrote segments, and offered general advice and counsel: Betty Collins, Michael Curran, Celeste Diehm, Denise Greene-Wilkinson, Kristin Nori, Linda Robinson, Teresa Sayre, and William Truesdale.

- The International Center for Leadership in Education for the use of the Rigor/Relevance Framework.

- The MetLife Foundation for the funding that enables NASSP to identify such schools as the three profiled in this book. Our sincere thanks also goes to the principals of the profiled schools: William Truesdale at Douglas Taylor School in Chicago, IL; Caroline Bloxom at Pocomoke Middle School in Pocomoke City, MD; and John O'Neill, former principal, and Karen Robinson, current principal of Forest Grove (OR) High School in Forest Grove.

- James R. Rourke, consultant and principal author, for his ability to synthesize and distill the thoughts of so many disparate voices.

We are also indebted to many who have contributed to the previous books in the *Breaking Ranks* series, including the Commission on the Restructuring of the American High School, the Carnegie Foundation for the Advancement of Teaching, Ted Sizer, the Education Alliance at Brown University, the Center for Secondary School Redesign, the Bill & Melinda Gates Foundation, the KnowledgeWorks Foundation, the MetLife Foundation, and the many individuals who shared their perspectives on this series.

The *Breaking Ranks* Framework AN OVERVIEW

Good ideas serve only as fodder for intellectual debate if they are not put to use…. Leadership requires that some people have the will and ability to act.

—*Breaking Ranks: Changing an American Institution*

The release of *Breaking Ranks: Changing an American Institution* in 1996 signaled the beginning of a new opportunity for principals to tackle the thorny issues involved in school reform. Designed by a broad range of practitioners and researchers who were keenly aware of the inner workings of high schools, it provided a statement of principles and a host of recommendations for school improvement. Many of the recommendations evolved from existing practices at middle level schools as well as the groundbreaking work of other practitioners and researchers who had tackled the topics individually or espoused various models of reform. Anyone familiar with the work of the Coalition of Essential Schools and Theodore Sizer's writing on the study of high schools, specifically *Horace's Compromise* (1984), will recognize commonalities in the areas of personalization, school and class size, instruction, and assessment. The influence of Ernest Boyer's 1983 work, *High School: A Report on Secondary Education in America*, relating to the interdisciplinary nature of curriculum, can also be seen in the recommendations. In addition, *A Nation at Risk* (National Education Commission on Time and Learning, 1983), *Prisoners of Time* (National Education Commission on Time and Learning, 1994), and *Turning Points* (Carnegie Council on Adolescent Development, 1989) all served to galvanize the debate about the need for reform and established substantive areas in which to undertake that reform.

Clearly the emphasis on a practitioner's view of reform struck a chord with principals and policymakers alike. Federal, state, and local policymakers, as well as accreditation organizations, have embraced many of the *Breaking Ranks* concepts and recommendations. Legislation, standards development, and other policy and structural initiatives are essential to systemic school improvement; however, doing the work of school improvement clearly falls upon the shoulders of educators—teachers, aides, assistant principals, principals, the central office personnel, and many others. To assist educators in doing the important work of improving schools, NASSP has published several companion pieces to address the "who" and "how" of implementing the "what" contained in *Breaking Ranks*. These works include:

- *Breaking Ranks II: Strategies for Leading High School Reform*
- *Breaking Ranks in the Middle: Strategies for Leading Middle Level Reform*
- *Breaking Ranks: A Field Guide for Leading Change*
- *10 Skills for Successful School Leaders*
- *Creating a Culture of Literacy*
- *Making the Math Curriculum Count.*

In the more than 15 years since principals, teachers, students, and other school leaders first came together to formulate the original recommendations, significant strides have been made to achieve that panel's goal of making schools more student centered by personalizing programs, support services, and intellectual challenges for each student. The many lessons about school improvement resulted in adjustments and refinements. This body of knowledge and experience—referred to hereafter as the "*Breaking Ranks* Framework"—will undoubtedly continue to adapt to changing expectations and further learning about what works and how it works in school communities.

This book, which is informed by research and proven practice, provides a detailed description of the *Breaking Ranks* Framework as it exists today in its evolved state: a framework that can support all schools in the K–12 continuum. This book builds upon what NASSP has learned since *Breaking Ranks II: Strategies for Leading High School Reform* and *Breaking Ranks in the Middle: Strategies for Leading Middle Level Reform* were released. In addition to incorporating and updating many of the key aspects of those books, this work also incorporates key components of two subsequent books in the series: *Breaking Ranks: A Field Guide for Leading Change* and *10 Skills for Successful School Leaders*. As a result, this big-picture view of the Framework points the reader to an abundance of resources and further practice materials that are available in the companion pieces.

Building Relationships Between Students and Ideas

On any given day, I think every adolescent is at-risk in some way.
—George Marnik

A significant component of what happens in schools—or in the business world for that matter—is social or personal. Accomplishments are based on a number of factors, including confidence, effort, knowledge, rewards, consequences, and satisfaction. Schools must appreciate that those variables and dozens of others change for students every day—and often many times during any given day—thereby potentially putting any student at risk. A thorough understanding of where a student is coming from is often difficult to reach, yet a school culture that systematically encourages that understanding will make great strides in helping students learn. Teacher-to-student and student-to-student relationships are tools within the classroom to generate excitement about ideas and learning.

Personalizing the school environment is an entry point to improving how a student interacts with and directs his or her own learning and encompasses the oversight, coaching, and motivational strategies that are associated with student-centered curriculum, instruction, and assessment. A student must have opportunities to develop a sense of belonging to the school, a sense of ownership over the direction of his or her learning, and the ability to recognize options and make choices that are based on his or her own experience and understanding of the options. **The *Breaking Ranks* Framework is designed to improve student performance by making learning personal**—by helping schools build better relationships within the school, opening the door to learning, and helping students build a more profound and productive relationship with ideas.

One Framework for Responsible K–12 School Improvement

How can one framework for school improvement work equally well in schools of different grade levels? No self-respecting educator would dare to espouse that schools serving elementary, middle level, or high school students should look the same. It boggles the mind to imagine high school students singing a "clean up" song commonly used in kindergarten or middle level students quietly sitting through a lecture given in an AP History class.

The attractiveness of the *Breaking Ranks* Framework is that it does not prescribe a specific model that a school must follow, but rather builds upon the individual school's data to assess strengths and identify needs so that a customized plan for school success can be developed. Regardless of grade level, all schools must address the three core areas of **collaborative leadership; personalizing your school environment;** and **curriculum, instruction, and assessment** to improve student performance. Only by addressing each of these three overlapping areas can improved student performance occur. Furthermore, it must be done in a manner that recognizes the specific academic and developmental needs—physical, social, emotional, and cognitive—of the students being served by the school. This is no easy task for any school. Schools with English language learners and other special populations have additional challenges. Consider the demands placed on a high school whose students' literacy skills range from beginning to college-level readers. The challenge is to engage each student at his or her level. Students have varying levels of knowledge and different learning styles that require teachers to use a host of teaching practices and techniques to engage each student on any given day.

All schools that hold true to the *Breaking Ranks* Framework will create a personalized, safe, inclusive, caring environment that is staffed with adults who understand and appreciate the unique characteristics of each age group. Those schools know that the teacher-student relationship is the key to learning but that personalizing the environment does little to promote improved student performance unless it is combined with high expectations and a rigorous and relevant curriculum supported by strong collaborative leadership. Educators in high-performing schools at all levels understand the unique development characteristics of students and use that knowledge "as a foundation for establishing school beliefs and core values and for setting leadership priorities that focus on learning and school improvement" (Clark & Clark, 2008, p. 1).

The *Breaking Ranks* Framework calls upon all schools to implement proven policies, practices, and structures to ensure that all students have a relationship with a trusted adult in the school and to eliminate the possibility of students remaining anonymous. Teaming, advisory programs, flexible schedules, opportunities for student leadership, parent and community involvement, and effective guidance services have, if properly implemented, all proven effective. Many such practices have come directly from reforms in middle level education and have proven effective at the elementary, middle, and high school levels. The *Breaking Ranks* Framework encourages each school to adopt these proven and accepted practices to ensure that students become engaged in highly challenging academic pursuits.

As the following sections attest, there are many challenges that differ between elementary level, middle level, and high schools, yet the *Breaking Ranks* Framework is comprehensive and flexible enough to implement at all levels. The Framework also makes sense as a way to further the alignment of policies and successful practices of schools across grade levels. It outlines ways for K–12 school leaders to engage in substantive conversations around alignment, transitions, and other school issues. To make the most of the flexibility of the *Breaking Ranks* Framework, principals and teacher leaders must understand and address the respective school and community cultures as well as the differences between sending and receiving schools and how the schools can collaborate.

At the Elementary Level...

One fish, two fish, red fish, blue fish.

—*Dr. Seuss*

Elementary schools have the distinctive challenge of working with students with the widest range of ages and developmental needs. Programs designed for the early grades (K–2) look quite different from those for the older children, and schools that are configured as K–8 have the additional responsibility of serving middle level students.

It is often said that the achievement gap begins before students enter school, and that is nowhere more apparent than in the early grades of an elementary school. Children begin school with a wide range of abilities and background experiences, and many low-income and minority students lag behind their peers in health, social, and emotional development; language and literacy skills; and mathematical thinking. This presents unique challenges to all elementary schools but especially those with a K–8 grade configuration. Imagine the challenge of keeping social development and cognitive growth in mind while helping some students *learn to read* while teaching others how to *read to learn*.

Because students start school with diverse backgrounds, elementary schools have the additional challenge of teaching the youngest students how to "do" school. Teachers in the early elementary grades must not only focus on basic academics but also address social and emotional needs by teaching students the skills needed for self-control, the language necessary to express their feelings and thoughts, and the skills required to interact with others in a positive manner. Such skills are often taught in upper elementary as well as to students just entering kindergarten. Each elementary student's learning needs must be identified and each must understand how to learn most effectively and advocate for him- or herself. In addition, students with disabilities are frequently in the early phases of the identification process and don't yet have IEPs, which means that elementary educators have the tough challenge of determining the best practices to meet each student's individual needs.

As students progress through the grades, their early school experience is crucial to their continued academic success. It is vital that adults who work with elementary level students remember that every child is different and begins school with different needs and motivations. Although some students begin school eager to learn and less rebellious than their older counterparts, schools face a major challenge in encouraging and working with those who struggle without dampening their self-esteem and enthusiasm for learning.

Providing students with quality instruction is a universal mission of all schools, but the wide range of student ages and development at the elementary level presents some unique challenges. The knowledge and skills needed to be an outstanding kindergarten teacher are different than those needed to successfully teach fifth graders, but both teachers must understand the needs of their students and the demands of the subjects they teach—quite a challenge, but also an opportunity to make connections across subjects. Leaders of elementary schools must be savvy about those differences and provide the professional development and support needed to ensure student success at every level, in every subject. Fortunately, students begin elementary school literally clinging to their parents, so many elementary schools have developed practices to leverage those high rates of parent participation. As students progress through the grades, however, parent involvement often decreases, so schools need to work diligently to solicit parent voice. Two of the stories in this book as well as the many stories and examples in *Breaking Ranks in the Middle* provide ideas that are applicable to elementary schools.

At the Middle Level...

> *At no other time in the life cycle are the changes of finding one's self and losing one's self so closely aligned.*
>
> —Erik Erikson

Those educators who work with middle level students, regardless of the grade configuration of the school, must realize that their school is neither a miniature high school nor an elementary school—it must be designed to meet the academic, social, and emotional needs of young adolescents. It's far too easy to forget that students entering the middle level are only five or six years removed from their teddy bears and those leaving are only a few short years away from the rigors of college.

Other than from birth to age three, 10- to 15-year-olds are experiencing the most rapid, significant changes of their lives—changes that are physical, social, emotional, and cognitive in nature. Schools that work successfully with middle level students understand and recognize that the students are seeking new levels of independence and can be highly peer centered; that the changes they are experiencing affect their thinking and behavior; and that each young adolescent is maturing on his or her own timeline—a student who appears to be physically mature may in reality be emotionally immature and a very concrete learner who finds it difficult to grasp abstract concepts.

This understanding of young adolescent development also affects decisions about curriculum, instruction, and assessment. Because adolescents live in the moment, the curriculum must capitalize on their personal interests and help them build connections between their lives and the world in which they live. The curriculum should be relevant, challenging, and interdisciplinary—and learning must be assessed through multiple measures, including real-life application and demonstration of knowledge and skills, and not solely based on state test scores. Instruction should be as varied and diverse as the students themselves; should take advantage of the young adolescent's need for movement and social interaction; and should be engaging, thought provoking, and interactive in nature.

But just as no two snowflakes are identical, neither are two middle level schools. Although the foundation of a school that serves middle level students must be based on knowledge of the young adolescent, school leaders must also take into account the unique nature of their school and their students and keep that nature at the heart of their decision making. As you put the *Breaking Ranks* Framework into practice at your middle level school, refer to the stories and examples of three unique schools in *Breaking Ranks in the Middle*.

At the High School Level...

> *Adolescence is a period of rapid changes. Between the ages of 12 and 17, for example, a parent ages as much as 20 years.*
>
> —Author Unknown

Compared with middle schools, high schools tend to be larger and more complex, which makes it easier for adults as well as students to become isolated from one another and focused on meeting their own individual needs. It is commonly said that high school teachers are a group of independent contractors brought together by a common parking lot.

Driven by the complexity of course content and the number of specialists required to teach myriad course offerings, the culture of high schools—particularly large high schools—can easily evolve into rigidly compartmentalized, adult- and content-focused subunits instead of a culture that is student and learning focused. Rather than developing a customized learning approach for every student, high schools may—and often do—lapse into what more closely resembles an impersonal assembly-line process.

High schools usually encompass more grade levels than middle schools, and they also have a wider range of student ages. High student mobility—the result of a number of societal factors—has resulted in interrupted schooling that causes some students to take more than four years to graduate. Today, it is not uncommon for high schools to have a significant number of 19-year-old seniors. The developmental difference between a 14-year-old ninth grader, who may more closely resemble a middle level student than a high school student, and a 19-year-old senior, who may look more like an adult than a high school student, is dramatic.

As dramatic are the differences between one high school and another. The practices that make learning personal within your school may differ from those in another school. Regardless, making that personal connection is critical. As you put the *Breaking Ranks* Framework into practice at your high school, refer to the stories and examples found in *Breaking Ranks II* for examples of three schools that used the Framework to successfully improve learning.

A Change in Culture

If schools are to improve—and they must—then school culture must evolve from an adult-focused, activity-oriented school environment to a student- and learning-focused culture. Schools must move from the assembly line to mass customization. Although each school is unique, high-performing schools—elementary, middle level, and high schools—will integrate the *Breaking Ranks* Framework into the culture of their schools.

School leaders must first recognize the critical role that a school's belief system plays in the sustainability of school improvement efforts. Second, they must carefully examine the process they are using to implement the change. Fullan (2005) described this type of change as the reculturing of schools:

> Sustainability is very much a matter of changes in culture: powerful strategies that enable people to question and alter certain values and beliefs as they create new forms of learning within and between schools, and across levels of the system. (p. 60)

Changing the attitudes, values, and beliefs that drive a school requires courage and effort. Underpinning this shift must be the core belief that each student should be challenged to achieve at high levels.

Expectations and Mind-Sets

The reality is that we can talk about culture and high achievement, and we can conduct high-quality professional development activities until we are blue in the face, but if teachers and other school leaders don't really believe or expect that each and every student can achieve at high levels, our efforts are doomed to failure.

In *Mindset*, Dweck (2006) noted that what people believe about success drives their behavior. One group, "fixed mind-set," believes that ability is something you either have or you don't and that ability is the best predictor of success. Those with a fixed mind-set worship talent and believe that no matter how hard one works, the level of achievement is limited by one's innate ability.

Dweck and other researchers have learned that the opposite is true: in the real world, work and effort create ability. Dweck discovered that some people have a "growth mind-set." They believe that success is the result of time, work, and deliberate practice. Her research has found that those with a growth mind-set were resilient learners who viewed problems as challenges and opportunities to learn. On the other hand, those with a fixed mind-set gave up easily and spent most of their time protecting their self-image. School leaders must do everything possible to help teachers acquire a growth mind-set. Once that is accomplished, our schools will be unstoppable.

Initiatives Affect Culture and Culture Affects Initiatives

Understanding that each initiative—and how it is implemented—could and should affect your school culture is essential. In the highly connected modern school, every action prompts a reaction or, more likely, multiple reactions. The key to the successful use of the *Breaking Ranks* Framework is to avoid the pick-and-choose mentality of, "Oh, I'll try this." Undertaking an initiative in the core area of personalizing your school environment without fully understanding and addressing how to support and make the most of it with accompanying modifications in the areas of collaborative leadership or curriculum, instruction, and assessment may prove to have unintended consequences. Consider what happens when a proven best practice that has worked well in many other schools is attempted in a school that implements the same practice poorly. The resulting failure demonstrates the importance of focusing on the "how." An initiative that is based on solid research, implemented within a collaborative process, and introduced with fidelity to the implementation procedures stands a greater chance of success and effectiveness. A focus on the collaborative process will help ensure that your school anticipates how one initiative will affect other core areas—an effect that may differ from another school implementing the same initiative.

Too often when implementing improvement initiatives, schools neglect to focus on the importance of altering school culture. A positive school culture can allow improvements to take hold, flourish, and be sustained. Changing culture requires more than being the first person with a great idea. Transformations do not take place until the culture of the school permits it—and no long-term significant change can take place without creating a culture to sustain that change. The question for education leaders at all levels is this: How can we foster cultural changes within schools so that we can lead improvement and enhance student learning? A great idea does not a great culture make; however, great leadership teams can have a lasting impact by creating a culture that challenges and educates each student.

The *Breaking Ranks* Framework is not a model or a mandate. The *Breaking Ranks* Framework is taking all of the programs, practices, and initiatives that provide incremental change and inserting them into a larger framework for improvement that alters the system and culture in fundamental ways. What is required is, according to Marzano, Waters, and McNulty (2005), "deep change [that] alters the system in fundamental ways, offering a dramatic shift in direction and requiring new ways of thinking and acting" (p. 66)—what they also refer to as "second-order change." What most schools instead produce is "first-order change": "incremental change [that] fine-tunes the system through a series of small steps that do not depart radically from the past" (Marzano, Waters, & McNulty, 2005, p. 66). The sad fact is that many of the changes being implemented are short lived with no lasting results. By focusing on the process as well as the reform initiatives, we hope to upend the oft-expressed sentiment coined by Irene Peter, "Just because everything is different doesn't mean anything has changed."

As a first step, the *Breaking Ranks* Framework prompts schools to ask some very basic questions about how the school is meeting the needs of each student. Subsequent focus is on creating a culture for the individual, the leadership team, and the school community that supports individual learning and an environment of success. The Framework at a Glance that follows illustrates the various components of the *Breaking Ranks* Framework. Each of these steps will be covered in greater detail in the remaining chapters.

Framework at a Glance

KEY QUESTION:

Why Does Your School Need to Improve?

***Breaking Ranks* Framework:**

How Well Does Your School Serve Each Student?

KEY QUESTION:

What Needs to Improve?

***Breaking Ranks* Framework:**

Nine cornerstones for improvement and
29 interconnected recommendations within
three core areas: Collaborative Leadership;
Personalizing Your School Environment;
Curriculum, Instruction, and Assessment

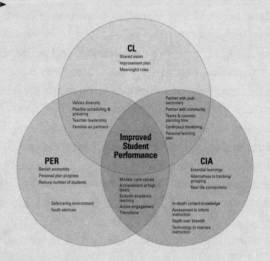

KEY QUESTION:

How Do We Improve Our School?

***Breaking Ranks* Framework:**

Six stages for systematic school improvement

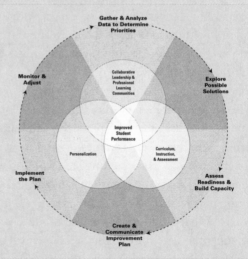

KEY QUESTION:

**Who? Do You and Your Team Have What
It Takes to Create a Culture for School
Improvement?**

***Breaking Ranks* Framework:**

Work to create a culture that will support improvement and examine your own leadership in these
10 skill areas:

Setting instructional direction	Organizational ability
Teamwork	Oral communication
Sensitivity	Written communication
Judgment	Developing others
Results orientation	Understanding own strengths and weaknesses

KEY QUESTION:
Why Does Your School Need to Improve?

Making learning personal for each student and learning how best to accomplish that is at the heart of the *Breaking Ranks* Framework. A school can only accomplish personalized learning within an environment that supports it. By analyzing how well your school is currently doing, your team can set benchmarks for future success. Your leadership team and others must begin by asking and answering important questions about how well your school serves each student. [See Appendix 1.]

KEY QUESTION:
What Needs to Improve?

To achieve the greatest gains in school improvement, the *Breaking Ranks* Framework calls on school leaders to focus simultaneously on three core areas:

- Collaborative leadership
- Personalizing your school environment
- Curriculum, instruction, and assessment.

Schools operate within the parameters of these three core areas, but as educators well know, there is considerable overlap and interdependence. As a complex institution, the school comprises many interlocking parts, as portrayed by the Venn diagram of the three core areas. Alter one element and you affect others. Because each school has its own dynamics, altering an element in one school may have profoundly different results than a similar change in another school. Therefore, the recommendations made in the *Breaking Ranks* Framework are best viewed not as a model but as a series of connected and interdependent proposals. Be forewarned: piecemeal change may lead to some immediate positive results, but it is not apt to be as effective or sustainable as efforts that reach into all parts of the system—in other words, systemic reform. Schools need more than tinkering.

At the foundation of this interconnected *Breaking Ranks* Framework lie nine cornerstones that should guide implementation of improvement initiatives. Think of them as the foundational concepts upon which the *Breaking Ranks* Framework is built:

- Leadership
- Professional Development
- Culture
- Organization
- Curriculum
- Instruction
- Assessment
- Relationships
- Equity.

KEY QUESTION:
How Do We Improve Our School?

Too often when implementing reforms, schools neglect to focus on the importance of altering school culture. Principals, teachers, and other school leaders are dedicated professionals who believe passionately in educating each student. Despite a long history of reforms, however, not every school has arrived at the point of serving each student. Every school leader has studied and reviewed plans or implemented reforms that appear, on the surface, to be thoughtful and to promise substantive impact. Yet when the plan becomes reality, the results are less significant than expected, the plan itself is too difficult to implement, or the resources needed are missing. In effect, those seeking to improve become so obsessed with the plan that they lose sight of the outcomes or the resulting changes cannot be sustained.

School improvement requires more than a great idea. Transformations do not take place until the culture of the school permits it—and no long-term, significant change can take place without creating a culture to sustain that change. Leaders at all levels must foster this transformed environment. A great idea does not create a great culture; however, great leadership teams acting on a good idea can have a lasting impact. The *Breaking Ranks* Framework provides a well-defined process that will not only help implement recommendations made in this book but also help to foster a culture of excellence and continuous improvement within your school.

> **Culture: the set of shared attitudes, values, goals, and practices that characterizes an institution or organization.**
>
> Source: Merriam Webster online

The process consists of six stages:

- Gather and analyze data to determine priorities
- Explore possible solutions
- Assess readiness and build capacity
- Create and communicate improvement plan
- Implement the plan
- Monitor and adjust.

Each of these stages is important to your improvement efforts. Neglecting any one will cause considerable harm to your school culture and individual improvement initiatives. Although you cannot neglect any stages, you may also not be able to address them sequentially. School improvement is a messy undertaking with no linear path to success. Engage in each of the six stages—you may cover each more than once—but adapt to your school's own circumstances and culture.

KEY QUESTION:

Who? Do You and Your Team Have What It Takes to Create a Culture for School Improvement?

One person alone cannot reach each student and help each student succeed. We need leaders who lead in many different ways and in numerous circumstances to implement the *Breaking Ranks* Framework. Principal, teacher, and student leadership are invaluable to the effort. Collaboration within grade levels, across grade levels, and across schools provides the backbone for the sustainability of the Framework. The old top-down, organizational chart–driven schools were good at sorting students for success, but they are simply too restrictive and too bureaucratic to respond to the needs of individual students. They were good at organizing but very bad at customizing. To reach every student, schools need to make learning personal for each individual.

Many middle schools have long operated with this backbone of collaboration in place. In the past 15 years, more high schools have begun to adopt similar practices, thanks in large part to school leaders and leadership teams who are willing to break ranks from the top-down norm. Those schools appreciate that school improvement can only occur if the culture permits it. Effective personal and team leadership can have a profound and lasting impact on school culture. Such teams operate under various names and in myriad formats—from leadership teams to professional learning communities. The names are not important but the collaboration is vital.

Principals and other school leaders must look within themselves to ensure that they have the necessary skills,

Implementation Success Relies on How

20% of Successful Implementation Relies on What	80% of Successful Implementation Relies on How
Differentiated instruction	Data collection and accurate analysis
Personal learning plans	Collaborative and distributed leadership
Advisories	Readiness assessment and ability to build capacity
Common planning time	
Flexible scheduling	
Activities/services tied to learning	Values alignment
K–16 continuity	Professional development
Small units	Project management
Real-world application	Communication and "buy-in"
	Role clarity and design
	Monitoring and adjustment

attitudes, and mind-sets to lead improvement. Leaders must believe that all students can achieve at high levels and that all staff members with the proper skills and mind-sets can support that achievement. For more than three decades, NASSP has been assessing and studying the skills of school leaders. As a result of that experience, analyses of the principalship, observation, and research, NASSP has identified 10 skills that encompass the bulk of what school leadership entails: setting instructional direction, teamwork, sensitivity, judgment, results orientation, organizational ability, oral communication, written communication, developing others, and understanding your own strengths and weaknesses.

Conscientious reflection will help you collaborate and delegate more effectively and be more appreciative of the contributions that others can make. Focused practice will enable you to become more effective in certain areas so that you can stop putting out fires (even those that you may have started or contributed to) and start reaping the benefits of collaborative planning. By constructively and systematically asking for focused feedback—in addition to the "How am I doing?" feedback—you can build consensus and culture, rather than dissension and controversy.

The 10 skills will be discussed within the context of the Framework; however, for a more in-depth look at how to improve your own skills, see the companion book *10 Skills for Successful School Leaders* (available from www.nassp.org).

Be Forewarned!

For the reader who is tempted to pick and choose a single strategy or section from this handbook or focus on one chapter that discusses a specific area of interest, be advised that implementing one or two recommendations is merely tinkering around the edges of school improvement and therefore ill-advised. Substantive improvement will only be successful and sustainable if it is continuous, involves an ongoing and rigorous analysis of the entire school's needs, and takes into account the interdependence of elements within a learning community. A best practice implemented in isolation may not be sustainable over time if it relies on other changes that are never implemented:

> In his research on schools that had improved rapidly and substantially, Cawelti (cited in Protheroe, 2011) found that multiple changes had been made and sustained over time. The schools that had not raised achievement were limited
>
> > by changing just one factor, such as schedule, teaching methods, or technology. Substantial improvement comes when a school is able to undertake several changes in an organized fashion and sustain and perfect them over a period of at least three to five years. (p. 2)

Substantial improvement requires a strategic vision. Successful schools

> do not simply write, sign, seal, and deliver an improvement plan…. They shape their solutions into a coordinated and thoughtful strategy to be implemented over a given period of time. [They] consider internal alignment. Do their proposed solutions (i.e., the changes they intend to make and new practices and programs they intend to implement) align with one another? Or do they conflict in such a way that one will undermine another? Do they add up to a coherent package? Do they offer the best fit for a school's particular culture and context? What additional variables, if left unaddressed, will offer roadblocks to any or all of the solutions?" (Jerald cited in Protheroe, 2011, p. 2).

Why?

CHAPTER 1

WHY CHANGE?
HOW WELL DOES YOUR SCHOOL SERVE EACH STUDENT?

Schools are often told to change but are rarely asked whether they believe they need to change. To truly change, the leadership team, faculty, and staff members must understand and support the need to change. Principals and other school leaders must ensure that this takes place by asking the right questions related to success and accountability.

Although schools are continually striving to improve, increased accountability for each student's learning, a changing world driven by technological innovation and complexity, and greater diversity of school communities have created a sense of urgency for school leaders. This confluence of events has signaled the end of equating a school's level of activity with its level of success—necessitating a shift in focus to outcomes. (See figure 1.1).

Figure 1.1
A Shift in Focus

Old School	New School
Managers	Instructional leaders
Adult-focused	Student-focused
Learning time is a constant	Learning time is a variable
Teaching	Learning
Seat time	Mastery
Bell curve	J curve
Covering content	Mastering essential learning
Access for all	Excellence for all
Individual star teachers	Teacher teams working together for each student's success
Status quo	Change

Equity of participation, the status quo, must be forced aside as equity of outcomes comes to the fore. Yet too often the outcomes still do not focus on the needs of each student within the school because leaders do not ask the right questions related to school success. According to the research from MetaMetrics regarding reading levels, current outcomes—or at least the reading skills required of today's students—have not kept pace with what is required of people in daily life. In fact, MetaMetrics research indicates that:

- The text complexity of K–12 textbooks has become increasingly "easier" over the last 50 years.
- The text demands of college and careers have remained consistent or increased over the same time period.
- As a result, there is a significant gap between students' reading abilities and the text demands of their postsecondary pursuits. Research shows that this gap is equal to a Lexile difference between grade 4 and grade 8 texts on the National Assessment of Educational Progress. (MetaMetrics, 2011a)

School leaders must generate the collective will to close that gap. Generally, people make difficult decisions about how they operate because they are required to do so or because they want to do so. In schools there are now clearly a number of external accountability mandates, many of which were designed to improve achievement for all students—including those who in the past were accepted as part of the "normal" failure curve. Disaggregated data requirements help ensure that all students receive the benefits of education, not simply that the overall school performance is "good enough."

> A Lexile measure is a valuable piece of information about either an individual's reading ability or the difficulty of the text.... If we know how well a student can read and how hard a specific book is to comprehend, we can predict how well that student will likely understand the book.
>
> MetaMetrics, 2011b

The most compelling mandate, however, is a moral one. Today, an 18-year old who is not college, career, and workplace ready is essentially sentenced to a lifetime of marginal employment. For the good of each student and for the good of our communities, each school must foster each student's success. Each student should be given the tools to discover the world of opportunity that awaits him or her and to investigate and acquire the knowledge and skills to be able to live and thrive in an increasingly global and competitive context. Schools must be inviting places and, in some cases, serve as the anchor for community improvement efforts.

In education, success cannot be a scarce commodity. In our schools, there can be no winners or losers. No one wins when students fail. Ensuring the success of each and every student is a win-win for everyone. If external mandates and moral equations are not enough, then selfish reasons should seal the deal. Most principals and teachers took their first step down the path to becoming educators because they wanted to make a difference in the lives of individuals by helping students acquire a love of learning. To make your dream become reality means helping each student realize his or her own dream. Their success is your success.

Many schools have implemented reforms that have resulted in improved student performance and their successes have shown policymakers that success on a grander scale is possible. Many schools, however, have failed to undertake reforms that have resulted in higher student achievement or have taken two steps forward and one step back. Time is of the essence; federal and state benchmarks must be met, but far more important, each minute wasted means less time is spent addressing the needs of students who are not achieving at acceptable levels. Millions of young people each year rely on principals and teachers to help them fulfill their dreams. Failure is not acceptable.

Asking the Right Questions

An exemplary school leader is one who acknowledges strengths but knows that there is much more to accomplish. Schools operating above certain benchmarks and schools that on average perform well enough to be highlighted in positive local news stories often don't have the "negative pressure incentive" to review how things could be better. In fact, those schools often are under pressure from the community to leave a good thing alone. But what is that "good thing" that should be left alone? Are you properly measuring that good thing—whatever it may be? Is it a good thing for each student, or is it a good thing just for the average student (as if such a person actually existed)? Measures of low, average, and high performance can be useful for some comparative analyses and for setting benchmarks; however, the real measure of performance is how well your school is meeting the academic needs of each student.

How do school communities turn students on to school—rather than off? If students do not want to attend schools, then the school environment may be the problem. Student thoughts, ideas, and perspectives need to be valued at every turn. Unfortunately, the student still exists who is made to feel "stupid" in school by peers or by a system that repeatedly reinforces weaknesses rather than providing the support needed for success. Why would a student want to return to a place where he is told, "Hey, according to our assessment, you're not smart enough, kid—and by the way, you are required to show up again tomorrow so you can be told that again." Personalized learning can help students reorient their thinking so that it doesn't devolve into "It's cool to be bad; it's not cool to be stupid." At the same time, schools must challenge advanced learners so they don't get the message "I know you weren't challenged yesterday or today, but according to the law, you're expected to be here tomorrow."

The most important part of any analysis is to ensure that the appropriate questions are being asked and answered—averages provide only one facet of any comprehensive analysis. To transform a school to the point at which it is academically excellent, responsive to the developmental needs of students, and socially equitable for the benefit of each student requires more thorough introspection from the school community. This quest for internal accountability will aid any effort to meet external district, state, and federal accountability mandates.

Following are questions that you and your school leadership team and the larger community should consider as you assess how well your school is meeting the needs of individual students. The questions are designed to address the individual rather than the "average"; however, if you are able to address the individual, chances are you will be pleasantly surprised by the "new average": a school more personalized in programs, support services, and intellectual rigor.

In order to prepare students to be lifelong learners ready for college, career, and citizenship, the National Forum seeks to make every middle grades school academically excellent, responsive to the developmental needs and interests of young adolescents, and socially equitable.

National Forum to Accelerate Middle-Grades Reform

How Well Does Your School Serve Each Student?

What practices are in place in your school to ensure that…

The school leadership team

- Establishes organizational structures and programs that foster personalization and banish anonymity?
- Reviews student data regularly to ensure that each student is on track to succeed at the next level of learning?

Each student

- Is engaged in a supportive relationship with at least one adult in the school who knows his or her aspirations, strengths, and weaknesses and helps him or her be successful?
- Is encouraged to take advantage of challenging courses and activities and receives the support needed to succeed in them?
- Provides input and feedback into the academic and social activities of the school?
- Participates with teachers and family in collaboratively planning his or her academic program?

Each teacher

- Communicates and maintains high expectations for each student's success and provides the instruction and support necessary to ensure that each student meets those expectations?
- Uses a variety of student data regularly to plan and deliver differentiated instruction and assessment that are developmentally appropriate for each learner?
- Serves as a learning facilitator and coach to engage each student in his or her learning and to accommodate individual learning needs?

Each family

- Participates meaningfully in the school's decision-making process?
- Participates as a critical partner with the school to ensure the success of each student's educational experience?
- Receives regular communications from the school with accommodations made for non-English speakers and special needs?

These questions serve as conversation starters for the school leadership team that is interested in exploring the degree to which the school serves each student equally well. The questions may be used by the leadership team to gauge the perceptions of groups of teachers, students, parents, and community members. They may also be used in mixed groups with the above constituencies represented.

Recording responses to the questions during the conversations is important to the next step of discussing the group's satisfaction or dissatisfaction with the responses. The satisfaction discussion helps provide information for the team to collaboratively begin shaping priorities for action.

A tool for gathering data for promoting the conversation around these questions is found in Appendix 1.

Always Room for Improvement

If everyone was satisfied with the responses gathered during the previous exercise as well as other measures of success (e.g., school climate and satisfaction surveys), then perhaps your school has already made the change from good to great. However, if the answers to this assessment indicate that there is room for improvement in your school, then you are in good company.

Despite the tremendous efforts and advances in meeting the needs of students at your school, much work remains. The next chapter will focus on what may need to change within your school.

Promoting Discussion Around "Why"
Why Change?

At the heart of the *Breaking Ranks* Framework is the foundational belief that learning must be personally meaningful to each student. The Framework also asserts that a school can only accomplish personalized learning by creating an environment that supports it. Actions required to create that supportive environment depend on each school's current characteristics. One way to assess your school in this area is to use the "How Well Does Your School Serve Each Student?" instrument found on page 151. Analyze data generated by this instrument and expand the conversation using the following questions:

- How do members of your school community (staff members, students, and parents) characterize their school (i.e. excellent, pretty good, or not good)?
- What differences and commonalities exist in the perceptions:
  - among school staff members?
  - among students?
  - among parents?
  - among groups in the school community?
- What factors contribute to disparate and common perceptions?
- What opportunities for improvement are revealed or affirmed by these data and the analysis conversations among school community members?
- What challenges for improvement are revealed or affirmed by these data and the analysis conversations among school community members?
- What constitutes a critical mass of the members of your school community to move forward with personalizing the learning for each student and creating the climate to support it?
- Beliefs drive behavior. What are the beliefs among your school community about your school's capacity and the need to serve the needs of each student equally well?

Making the Case for Gauging School Climate

To help schools draw staff members, students, and parents into a collaborative school improvement process, NASSP has created the Comprehensive Assessment of School Environment (CASE)—a series of perception surveys using the concepts in the *Breaking Ranks* Framework. All survey items are focused around the three core areas of *Breaking Ranks:* collaborative leadership; personalization; and curriculum, instruction, and assessment.

CASE is designed to:

- Collect data about student, teacher, and parent satisfaction with a school's environment and culture
- Identify the school's strengths and areas for improvement
- Assist in designing a school improvement plan using the *Breaking Ranks* process circle and support planning, including budget decisions.

Visit www.nassp.org/case for more information.

What?

CHAPTER 2

WHAT NEEDS TO IMPROVE?
CORNERSTONES OF SUCCESS

As you engage in thoughtful conversations within your school and community to define and implement a vision of improvement, keep in mind that your challenge is not educating students, rather it is educating each student. At the heart of any family's vision is one constant—not the success of the amorphous "all students" but the success of "our son" or "our daughter." Your school's vision must take each family's vision to heart. Bringing that to reality will require a strategic plan for what needs to change—a plan that incorporates academic excellence, developmental responsiveness, and social equity at every opportunity. Remember, a vision will remain simply a vision unless your school is willing to embark on significant changes to bring it to life.

There is no template for what a *Breaking Ranks* school should look like because school culture differs from community to community; however, the *Breaking Ranks* Framework rests upon nine cornerstones and a host of recommendations intended to improve and personalize schools. Those cornerstones and recommendations have been gleaned and refined from decades of experience, extensive research by practitioners and academics alike, and the earlier versions of *Breaking Ranks*. In fact, considerable refinement has taken place within the last 15 years since the earliest recommendations were made. But throughout, the one consistent theme of the *Breaking Ranks* Framework has always been that each school, each principal, and each teacher must make learning personal for each student.

Note the words *learning* and *personal*. Learning must be at the heart of everything schools do; making it personal doesn't mean to focus exclusively on developmental factors or to give students a summer camp experience at the expense of academics. Instead, the *Breaking Ranks* Framework is a challenge to each school to understand each student and how he or she learns best, something that can only be accomplished by knowing each student well. Just as any parent with more than one child understands that one tactic may work for one child but not another, schools have begun to get away from the assembly-line mentality. By making learning personal, a school can develop the right structures and tactics to challenge each student and engage him or her in learning.

> **Personalization in Two Parts**
> 1. The human element: strengthening relationships among people, fostering an environment conducive to learning.
> 2. The learning element: establishing relationships between students and ideas—how the student interacts and directs his or her own learning.

Student Engagement Is More Than Participation

As Schmoker (2011) pointed out in *Focus*, "Teachers routinely call on students who raise their hands throughout the course of most lessons (vivid confirmation that teachers aren't clear on the most critical elements of a good lesson)" (p. 14). Schmoker knows that when teachers regularly call on students who raise their hands, only about 10% of the students in that classroom will be actively engaged. *Engagement* is defined as "students actively interacting with the teacher or other students relative to the content of the lesson." Schmoker goes on to praise Robert Marzano's insistence that "we must ensure, as we lecture, that all are engaged—not just those who raise their hands. We must ensure that every student is responding, multiple times, to questions throughout the lecture."

Creating Challenge

If you believe that on any given day every student is "at risk" in some way and that your school has the ability to help students address some risks, then you will prefer a school in which each student is personally challenged to develop intellectually, socially, ethically, and physically. But how does one create systems to ensure that each student is personally challenged?

The *Breaking Ranks* Framework creates structures and promotes behaviors that strengthen relationships among people—students, teachers, staff members, families, and the larger community. It also fosters another important facet of personalization: relationships between students and ideas—how the student interacts and directs his or her own learning with the oversight, coaching, and motivational strategies associated with student-centered curriculum, instruction, and assessment.

To make learning personal each school community must review its strategies, actions, initiatives and culture in three core areas:

- Collaborative leadership
- Curriculum, instruction, and assessment
- Personalizing your school environment.

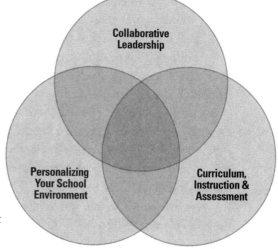

Collaborative Leadership

Collaborative leadership relies on the outstanding skills and contributions from many individual leaders working together to develop a plan and a process for school improvement. Principals and other leaders must systematically create opportunities for participation by all stakeholders in developing a plan that is values driven and data informed. It is very difficult for someone to oppose an improvement initiative if you supply data and explain how the initiative is designed to benefit each student. The recommendations and strategies in this chapter will offer a number of substantive opportunities for your school to develop collaborative leadership.

As you ask yourself how you can use the *Breaking Ranks* Framework to bring about school improvement where others have failed, focus special attention on collaborative leadership. Remember that in many cases it was not a lack of effort that killed reforms. More often than not it was a failure to address the culture or a failure of process—or both. Do not underestimate the importance of having a school leadership team that understands the change process, uses data to justify the need for change, gets others involved in the process, and provides the necessary professional development to implement, assess, and sustain the improvement:

> It is clear that the school's culture can either support or impede improvement efforts. In schools that he studied, Cawelti (1999) found teamwork to be a way of life. People on teams "meet regularly to examine assessment results and plan instruction based on these results, to plan cooperative instructional activities, and to communicate and solve problems" (p. 63). Researchers from the Consortium on Chicago School Research discussed the importance of what they call "relational trust" to school improvement efforts, with Bryk (2010) characterizing relational trust as a "lubricant for organizational change" (p. 27). Sebring, Allensworth, Bryk, Easton, and Luppescu (2006) advised that

> > knowing and trusting one another makes it easier to reach consensus about priorities, fosters a sense of teamwork and professional community, and provides an environment where it is safe to experiment and even to fail. With a sense that "we're all in this together," the staff [moves] forward with conviction, and if plans go awry, they know they can recover. (p. 46)

> Research on schools that are successfully engaged in improvement efforts identified the importance of meaningful opportunities for professional growth that are aligned with the improvement plan. In successful schools, teachers set staff development priorities that are keyed to their vision of the reform goals in their schools. In some instances, teacher teams developed strategic plans that allowed sustained, coherent immersion in an area. Forsaking a disjointed series of one-session workshops, teachers sought the expertise and time necessary to acquire, implement, and reflect on innovations on an ongoing basis (Quellmalz et al., 1995). (Protheroe, 2011, pp. 3–4)

Fullan (cited in Mourshed, Chijioke, & Barber, 2010) explained the power of collaborative practice, what he terms "collective capacity" in this manner:

> Collective capacity is when groups get better—school cultures, district cultures and government cultures. The big collective capacity and the one that ultimately counts is when they get better conjointly—collective, collaborative capacity, if you like. Collective capacity generates the emotional commitment and the technical expertise that no amount of individual capacity working alone can come close to matching.... The power of collective capacity is that it enables ordinary people to accomplish extraordinary things—for two reasons. One is that knowledge about effective practice becomes more widely available and accessible on a daily basis. The second reason is more powerful still—working together generates commitment. Moral purpose, when it stares you in the face through students and your peers working together to make lives and society better, is palpable, indeed virtually irresistible. The collective motivational well seems bottomless. The speed of effective change increases exponentially. (p. 74)

Collaborative practice is all about teachers and school leaders working together to develop effective (defined) instructional practices, studying what works well in classroom, and doing so both with rigorous attention to detail and a commitment to improving not only one's own practice but also that of others. Collaborative practice is the method by which a school system "hardwires" the values and beliefs implicit in its system into a form manifest in day-to-day teaching practice.

Every profession has a standard set of defined practices. Physicians, dentists, airline pilots, and accountants all have agreed-upon standards of practice. Likewise, schools have defined discipline practices, arrival practices, dismissal practices, dress practices, testing practices, computer use practices, and cafeteria practices. Ironically, very few schools have a set of defined instructional practices relating to teaching and learning.

For school improvement efforts to be effective, they must affect the classroom in a positive way. Instructional strategies that worked well in a time in which schools sorted students for success fall short in a time in which we expect all students to achieve at high levels.

Individual teachers, no matter how talented they are, cannot raise the performance of all students in a school. For example, to significantly improve literacy skills, purposeful reading and writing must occur in each classroom each day. Reaching each student demands that everyone in the school pull together their collective experience and intelligence as well as their skills sets. It is the job of school leaders to ensure that everyone is working together.

Even with fewer resources, schools are expected to make significant improvements in student performance and in a short period of time. Because time is of the essence, insisting on building teacher capacity one teacher at a time will never get schools where they need to go. Instead, school leaders must focus on building the collective capacity of the entire staff to deliver quality instruction. The key to raising the collective capacity of the staff is to collaboratively develop a set of defined instructional practices that are agreed upon and used consistently throughout the school. School leaders can use defined instructional practices to build the collective capacity of teachers to actively engage students and improve student achievement.

Ultimately, we want our teachers to say, "It is easy to get things done in this school because all the teachers are working together." That will never happen by accident.

Sustaining Improvement

Sustainability of improvement also requires leaders to grow leaders. "Each one teach one" expresses the responsibility of individuals in an organization to pass on and perpetuate sets of desired skills, behaviors, and customs important to the organization. Teaching someone else is an effective strategy for ensuring the retention of the knowledge or a skill. If this is true, sharing one's capacity for positive leadership and effective behavior would seem to contribute to improving schools in several ways.

Everyone has a backup. Too frequently one person is given sole responsibility for an important task in school. Over time, that person becomes indispensable to the operation of the school because no one else can do the important task. But, of course, no one is indispensable. Every member of the school staff should be responsible for developing the capacity of at least one person to meet his or her responsibilities, especially ones that are essential to the operation of the enterprise. This is consistent with the *Breaking Ranks* principles of collaborative leadership and contributes to building ownership among school community members.

Many heads are better than one. When principals collaborate with assistant principals, teacher leaders, aspiring principals, veteran teachers, and new teachers to improve student learning, it enriches all involved. Shared decision making takes longer, but it taps into the collective intelligence of the entire staff. Sharing responsibilities gives everyone opportunities to learn from others whose perspectives, knowledge, and skills are different from their own. A synergy builds from those collaborative conversations. Shared ownership of results is a powerful product of school community members teaching one another their best professional practices.

Maintain, sustain, grow. Many of us have seen a strong principal turn a poorly performing school into a successful one and then for one reason or another leave the school. Too often, we have also seen the improvements and successful performance decline rapidly upon the strong leader's departure. To help ensure that improvements are sustained and become a part of a positive student-centered school culture, leaders build the capacity of others to continue to move forward. Shared leadership builds a sense of efficacy in the staff members who come to see that continuous improvement is within their power and is their responsibility. Sustaining good performance must include developing the belief that continuous growth is essential to providing the best possible learning culture for each student.

Everyone plans for succession. Succession planning is a much-overlooked responsibility of leadership. Every leader in a school should have a successor. Every department chair, every team leader, every coach, and every sponsor should be actively mentoring a successor. The principal should ask, "If you could not attend a meeting, who would you send in your place?" That person is your successor! Teach him or her. Succession planning is essential to the sustained success and continued development of any organization. The process involves the identification and development of individuals within the organization who have potential for success in other roles in the organization. Typically "succession planning" refers to leadership positions. Principals have a responsibility to identify individuals who have leadership potential and to encourage, support, and coach them so that they build their capacity to lead successfully in the school. The "everyone has a backup" concept contributes to succession planning across the organization. Succession planning also contributes to maintaining, sustaining, and growing for continuous improvement.

Curriculum, Instruction, and Assessment

Successfully implementing a rigorous curriculum relies on engaged students who are willing to be challenged and to challenge themselves. When you look to establish a rigorous curriculum, it should:

1. Be authentic
   - ❏ Be product-oriented
   - ❏ Contain quality standards that are set in advance
   - ❏ Require application of skills
   - ❏ Be open-ended and problem-based
2. Be thoughtful and reflective
   - ❏ Require analysis, synthesis, evaluation
   - ❏ Have multiple outcomes
   - ❏ Require new ways of thinking
   - ❏ Be judged on quality criteria and evidence
3. Create dissonance in learner
   - ❏ Use real-world problems
   - ❏ Have no clear answer, only high-quality ones

❏ Require new behavior, skills, and learning

❏ Entertain the possibility of failure

4. Be individualized

❏ Permit student to pursue interests

❏ Be differentiated

❏ Provide support

❏ Require self-evaluation

Creating relationships between students and ideas requires adults to understand students. For example, addressing the needs of students of various levels requires an excellent understanding of where they are and meeting their needs with appropriate practices. The challenge for schools is to align curriculum, instruction, and assessment so that students know what standards they need to meet and receive the support to become engaged in achieving those standards.

Figure 2.1

Purposes and Indicators of Personalized Learning

Purposes	
Increase student motivation	Banish anonymity from school life
Help students control their future	Assess progress toward standards
Connect families to student learning	Connect academic and applied learning
Celebrate student achievement	Encourage college aspirations
Connect each student with a caring adult	Promote reflection and reevaluation
Relates student work to standards	Assess basic skills (speaking and writing)
Explore noncurricular options	Explore career choices
Support identify formation	Demonstrate personal talents
Initiate lifelong learning	Extend range of academic choice
Increase self-awareness	Evaluate content acquisitions
Emphasize applications of knowledge	Recognize nonschool achievements

Indicators
Personalized learning begins with individual interests so that each student becomes engaged in learning.
The achievement of standards for all students is promoted.
Teachers get to know each student's strengths, weaknesses, and interests.
Adults in the school model and benefit from stronger professional and student relationships.
Students learn to set goals and measure success for themselves against common standards.
Reaching all students depends on reaching each one.

Source: Adapted from DiMartino, J., Clarke, J., & Wolk, D. (2003). *Personalized learning: Preparing high school students to create their futures.* Lanham, MD: Scarecrow Press.

What does that support look like? Significant effort should be exerted to generate excitement about learning. Making learning personal is about the relationships between students and ideas—how the student interacts and directs his or her own learning with the oversight, coaching, and motivational strategies associated with student-centered curriculum, instruction, and assessment. Without structural changes and changes in classroom practice that promote student self-awareness and exploration, personalized learning cannot flourish. Personalized learning—building the relationships between students and ideas—is related to, yet distinct from, the efforts to personalize the school environment which are more about building relationships between people. (See figure 2.1.)

Personalizing Your School Environment

Although some students might be able to make it through the childhood, young adolescence, and the teenage years despite the lack of personal connections, most students require a supportive environment—some more than others. Creating that environment is essential if a school is to bring learning to fruition for each student.

Each school must provide students with opportunities to develop a sense of belonging to the school, a sense of ownership over the direction of their learning, and the ability to recognize options and make choices based on their own experiences and understanding of the options. The following is a working definition of *personalization*:

> A learning process in which schools help students assess their own talents and aspirations, plan a pathway toward their own purposes, work cooperatively with others on challenging tasks, maintain a record of their explorations, and demonstrate their learning against clear standards in a wide variety of media, all with the close support of adult mentors and guides. (Clarke, 2003, p. 15)

Personalizing your school environment sets the stage for learning by addressing the school environment, climate, and culture with certain practices. Those practices are designed to prevent students from remaining anonymous; allow teachers to appreciate and foster each student's abilities, aspirations, and interests; encourage students to exercise and practice personal and social responsibility, decision making, and communication skills; and offer students opportunities to demonstrate their academic, athletic, musical, dramatic, and other accomplishments in a variety of ways. Implementing structural changes to foster these practices provides the "shell" in which productive interaction—relationships—can occur systematically.

What to Tackle First?

Scholars, school leadership teams, and management experts have long struggled with the question of what to tackle first: Collaborative leadership? Curriculum, instruction, assessment? Personalization? Without minimizing the importance of the debate, suffice it to say that the three are highly interconnected and change is needed in all three areas. In addition, modifications to culture must occur before change truly becomes effective. Unfortunately, schools don't have the luxury of sequentially addressing culture then addressing student learning needs—they must "build the plane while it is in flight." The process—the how of improvement—can have a profound effect on your culture, for better or worse. Each school will approach the challenge from a different perspective depending on factors specific to its situation.

Although the approach may vary from school to school, the following cornerstones should be at the center of all initiatives in each school embracing the *Breaking Ranks* Framework:

- Leadership
- Professional development
- Culture
- Organization
- Curriculum
- Instruction
- Assessment
- Relationships
- Equity.

These interrelated cornerstones form the foundation for improving the performance of each student in your school. Each of these cornerstones—and their underlying recommendations—will be the focus of the next nine pages. They form the heart of "what" to change. Reflecting the interrelated nature of the schooling enterprise and the fact that changing one variable will have an impact in other areas, many of the underlying recommendations repeat. For example, "vision" is required for leadership as well as professional development and most of the other cornerstones. While this may seem repetitive, it provides a constant reminder of the interconnectedness as well as a "one-stop" place to see the associated recommendations for those who may be reviewing one cornerstone, such as "organization," as a group. Although all cornerstones must be addressed in a combined effort, to engage in conversations about all nine cornerstones at once would be impractical at best. Given the import and depth of impact of the underlying ideas, it would be just as easy to say "Read the book and react." To aid your exploration, the following pages are organized in this manner:

- Each page has one of the cornerstones, a brief description, and the *Breaking Ranks* Framework recommendations that are the "what" of improvement.
- Following the nine pages of cornerstones is the complete list of 29 recommendations organized by core area.
- These recommendations are further defined by the benefits, strategies, challenges, and progress measures for each recommendation (pp 42–71). This level of depth will be instrumental in helping your school discuss how best to implement each recommendation. Extensive discussions should take place about these recommendations.

> **Teaching versus Learning**
> Teaching involves demonstrating skills and presenting knowledge, but learning does not occur until the students engage and understand.
> Source: ICLE

Leadership

Leadership practices must be collaborative, inclusive, and mission driven and value the voice of all members of the school community. To foster effective learning and accountability, teachers, parents, students, and other stakeholders must be given substantive opportunities for involvement in the decision-making process and its continual monitoring. As you review the recommendations below, it should become clear that much of the school's collective energy necessarily revolves around enhancing leadership capacity and that the attitudes, values, beliefs, and dispositions of leaders at all levels are critical to success. While committing to a shared vision, leaders should provide direction and encourage a diversity of perspectives representative of the school community.

Recommendations

- The principal leads in developing, articulating, and committing to a shared vision and mission focused on student success. [See p. 42]
- The school provides meaningful decision-making roles for staff members, students, and parents. [p. 43]
- All members of the school community actively collaborate to develop and implement the agreed-upon learning goals and improvement plan. [p. 44]
- Teachers and teacher teams provide the leadership that is essential to student success. [p. 45]
- Each staff member develops a personal learning plan (PLP) that is aligned with the school improvement plan. [p. 46]
- The school values diversity and fosters an array of viewpoints, perspectives, and experiences. [p. 47]
- The school develops partnerships with individuals, organizations, community agencies, and businesses to support its mission. [p. 49]
- The school, in addition to its continuous monitoring of progress and yearly reporting, will convene a broad-based panel to conduct an in-depth assessment and present their findings to the public at least once every three years. [p. 50]
- The school collaboratively develops and reviews with each student a personal plan for progress that promotes ownership of the student's learning goals and provides strategies for achieving high standards. [p. 54]
- The school and students' families are partners in fostering the academic, intellectual, social and emotional success of each student. [p. 57]
- The school advocates and models a set of core values that are essential in a democratic and civil society. [p. 58]
- The school coordinates with community agencies in the delivery of social, physical, and mental health services to meet the needs of students and their families. [p. 59]
- The school fosters collaboration to improve student performance through such structures as teacher teams and regularly scheduled common planning time. [p. 62]
- Teachers promote active engagement of each student in his or her own learning through coaching and facilitating. [p. 69]
- The school ensures a smooth academic and social transition for each student from grade to grade and school to school. [p. 70]

Professional Development

Professional development must be individualized; aligned with the school improvement goals; and designed to increase knowledge of content, skills in instruction and assessment, and understanding of the developmental characteristics of students. Research indicates that effective professional development is continual, ongoing, connected, and job embedded. School improvement relies on the personal commitment of each principal, teacher, and staff member to increase his or her own capacity to teach, to lead, and to understand the importance of the nuances of "how" to change, not just "what" to change. Process is critical. A well-defined and implemented plan for improvement can lead to sustainability if the culture is changed and the community "buy-in" required to implement change is not overlooked. As you review the predominantly structural-related recommendations below, consider the professional development that will be required to foster a healthy culture and effective processes to implement those structural changes.

Recommendations

- All members of the school community actively collaborate to develop and implement the agreed-upon learning goals and improvement plan. [p. 44]

- Each staff member develops a personal learning plan (PLP) that is aligned with the school improvement plan. [p. 46]

- The school values diversity and fosters an array of viewpoints, perspectives, and experiences. [p. 47]

- The school develops partnerships with postsecondary institutions to enhance learning for students and adults. [p. 48]

- The school fosters collaboration to improve student performance through such structures as teacher teams and regularly scheduled common planning time. [p. 62]

- Teachers plan and deliver challenging, developmentally appropriate lessons that actively engage each student; emphasize depth over breadth; and develop skills, such as creative and critical thinking, problem solving, decision making, and communication. [p. 66]

- Teachers design and use formative and summative assessments to inform instruction, advance learning, accommodate individual learning needs, and monitor student progress. [p. 67]

- Each educator possesses pedagogical expertise, a broad academic foundation, in-depth content knowledge in the subjects taught, and an understanding of the developmental needs of his or her students. [p. 68]

- Teachers promote active engagement of each student in his or her own learning through coaching and facilitating. [p. 69]

Culture

The culture of the school must support and be supported by attitudes, values, and behaviors that promote high expectations and a belief that each student is capable of achieving personal and academic success. Creating a culture of high expectations and accountability often requires fundamental changes in the school's existing culture, an undertaking that can only be achieved and sustained with reflection and a well-defined and implemented process.

Recommendations

- The principal leads in developing, articulating, and committing to a shared vision and mission focused on student success. [p. 42]

- The school provides meaningful decision-making roles for staff members, students, and parents. [p. 43]

- All members of the school community actively collaborate to develop and implement the agreed-upon learning goals and improvement plan. [p. 44]

- Teachers and teacher teams provide the leadership that is essential to student success. [p. 45]

- The school values diversity and fosters an array of viewpoints, perspectives, and experiences. [p. 47]

- The school creates a safe, caring environment characterized by interactions between adults and students that convey high expectations, support, and mutual respect. [p. 55]

- The school and students' families are partners in fostering the academic, intellectual, social, and emotional success of each student. [p. 57]

- The school advocates and models a set of core values that are essential in a democratic and civil society. [p. 58]

- The school fosters collaboration to improve student performance through such structures as teacher teams and regularly scheduled common planning time. [p. 62]

- The school's instructional practices and organizational policies demonstrate its belief that each student—with work, effort, and support—can achieve at high levels. [p. 65]

- Teachers promote active engagement of each student in his or her own learning through coaching and facilitating. [p. 69]

Organization

The school's organizational structures and schedules must be flexible, promote collaboration, and accommodate teaching and learning strategies that are consistent with the ways students in various stages of development learn. Teacher collaboration and teacher teaming provide excellent opportunities to accomplish learning objectives and share strategies. As you review the recommendations below, consider what structures or practices your school has in place to foster teacher collaboration. Also consider how those structures help everyone view learning time as a valuable commodity—a commodity that can be distributed flexibly so that teachers are not confined in their quest to design lessons with the highest impact on learning.

Recommendations

- All members of the school community actively collaborate to develop and implement the agreed-upon learning goals and improvement plan. [p. 44]

- Teachers and teacher teams provide the leadership that is essential to student success. [p. 45]

- The school establishes structures and practices to banish anonymity and individualize the learning experience for each student. [p. 51]

- The school reduces the number of students each teacher is responsible for teaching to ensure that each student receives high-quality instruction, feedback, and support. [p. 53]

- The school implements scheduling and student-grouping practices that are flexible, meet each student's needs, and ensure successful academic growth and personal development. [p. 56]

- The school offers alternatives to tracking and ability grouping while maintaining the flexibility to appropriately support and challenge each student. [p. 61]

- The school fosters collaboration to improve student performance through such structures as teacher teams and regularly scheduled common planning time. [p. 62]

- The school supports and extends academic learning and personal development for each student through such structures as service learning, community service, and student activities. [p. 64]

Curriculum

The school's curriculum must be challenging, standards-based, aligned K–12, relevant, and exploratory and must build connections between subject areas. Students, teachers, and parents must have a clear idea of what students are expected to learn every day, every week, and every year in order to progress and succeed in school. Curriculum mapping and collaboration between grades and schools will help ensure that teachers have the information they need to design appropriate and nonrepetitive lessons and that all stakeholders understand the materials upon which students will be assessed. As you review the recommendations below, consider the degree to which parents at your school believe the curriculum is challenging, relevant, well articulated, and well communicated.

Recommendations

- The principal leads in developing, articulating, and committing to a shared vision and mission focused on student success. [p. 42]
- All members of the school community actively collaborate to develop and implement the agreed upon learning goals and improvement plan. [p. 44]
- The school develops partnerships with postsecondary institutions to enhance learning for students and adults. [p. 48]
- The school reduces the number of students each teacher is responsible for teaching to ensure that each student receives high-quality instruction, feedback, and support. [p. 53]
- The school collaboratively develops and reviews with each student a personal plan for progress that promotes ownership of the student's learning goals and provides strategies for achieving high standards. [p. 54]
- The school advocates and models a set of core values that are essential in a democratic and civil society. [p. 58]
- The school identifies essential learnings and the standards for mastery in all subjects. [p. 60]
- The school connects its curriculum to real-life applications and extends learning opportunities beyond its campus. [p. 63]
- The school supports and extends academic learning and personal development for each student through such structures as service learning, community service, and student activities. [p. 64]
- Each educator possesses pedagogical expertise, a broad academic foundation, in-depth content knowledge in the subjects taught, and an understanding of the developmental needs of his or her students. [p. 68]
- The school ensures a smooth academic and social transition for each student from grade to grade and school to school. [p. 70]

Instruction

Instruction must be differentiated, challenging, and actively engaging and take into account the academic, social, and developmental needs of each student. A well-designed and seamless curriculum without appropriate instruction provides few results to all but the most self-motivated and unique students. Effective instruction for each student requires teachers to understand and engage students differently. Consequently, teachers must be content experts as well as experts at teaching and using various strategies and technologies to help students learn—not simply to minimal levels but to the greatest extent possible.

Recommendations

- The principal leads in developing, articulating, and committing to a shared vision and mission focused on student success. [p. 42]

- All members of the school community actively collaborate to develop and implement the agreed-upon learning goals and improvement plan. [p. 44]

- The school reduces the number of students each teacher is responsible for teaching to ensure that each student receives high-quality instruction, feedback, and support. [p. 53]

- The school implements scheduling and student grouping practices that are flexible, meet each student's needs, and ensure successful academic growth and personal development. [p. 56]

- The school offers alternatives to tracking and ability grouping while maintaining the flexibility to appropriately support and challenge each student. [p. 61]

- The school fosters collaboration to improve student performance through such structures as teacher teams and regularly scheduled common planning time. [p. 62]

- The school's instructional practices and organizational policies demonstrate its belief that each student, with work, effort, and support, can achieve at high levels. [p. 65]

- Teachers plan and deliver challenging, developmentally appropriate lessons that actively engage each student; emphasize depth over breadth; and develop skills, such as creative and critical thinking, problem solving, decision making, and communication. [p. 66]

- Each educator possesses pedagogical expertise, a broad academic foundation, in-depth content knowledge in the subjects taught, and an understanding of the developmental needs of his or her students. [p. 68]

- Teachers promote active engagement of each student in his or her own learning through coaching and facilitating. [p. 69]

- The staff and students use current technology to improve instruction, enhance individualized learning, and facilitate management and operations. [p. 71]

Assessment

Assessment must be varied, an integral part of the learning process, and used regularly to ensure that instruction promotes student success. Assessment should be systematic and balanced and provide opportunities for students to see success. Assessment certainly has its place in the arena of accountability, but if learning is the real goal, effective assessment should be used systematically by each teacher on a daily basis to help gauge how well the lessons are being understood. As you review the recommendations below, consider how school leaders can help ensure that teachers are changing instruction on the basis of regular assessments and how technology can help improve and supplement traditional methods.

Recommendations

- The principal leads in developing, articulating, and committing to a shared vision and mission focused on student success. [p. 42]
- All members of the school community actively collaborate to develop and implement the agreed-upon learning goals and improvement plan. [p. 44]
- The school reduces the number of students each teacher is responsible for teaching to ensure that each student receives high-quality instruction, feedback, and support. [p. 53]
- The school implements scheduling and student-grouping practices that are flexible, meet each student's needs, and ensure successful academic growth and personal development. [p. 56]
- The school offers alternatives to tracking and ability grouping while maintaining the flexibility to appropriately support and challenge each student. [p. 61]
- The school fosters collaboration to improve student performance through such structures as teacher teams and regularly scheduled common planning time. [p. 62]
- Teachers design and use formative and summative assessments to inform instruction, advance learning, accommodate individual learning needs, and monitor student progress. [p. 67]
- Each educator possesses pedagogical expertise, a broad academic foundation, in-depth content knowledge in the subjects taught, and an understanding of the developmental needs of his or her students. [p. 68]
- The staff and students use current technology to improve instruction, enhance individualized learning, and facilitate management and operations. [p. 71]

Relationships

The school's structures, programs, and practices must be designed to build healthy, respectful relationships among all members of the school's community and ensure that each student is well known by at least one adult. The importance of relationships to learning is often overlooked, yet how many of us can point to a teacher, an adviser, a principal, or a coach who made a profound difference in not only our academic lives but also in our overall life course? Every student needs a sounding board as well as someone whom they trust to be their advocate in the academic and personal realms. As you review the recommendations below, consider not only how your school promotes effective and caring student to teacher relationships but also how your culture promotes positive teacher to teacher and other relationships. Open and honest school-based relationships are fundamental to building a culture of excellence.

Recommendations

- The school provides meaningful decision-making roles for staff members, students, and parents. [p. 43]

- All members of the school community actively collaborate to develop and implement the agreed-upon learning goals and improvement plan. [p. 44]

- The school values diversity and fosters an array of viewpoints, perspectives, and experiences. [p. 47]

- The school establishes structures and practices to banish anonymity and individualize the learning experience for each student. [p. 51]

- The school reduces the number of students each teacher is responsible for teaching to ensure that each student receives high-quality instruction, feedback, and support. [p. 53]

- The school collaboratively develops and reviews with each student a personal plan for progress that promotes ownership of the student's learning goals and provides strategies for achieving high standards. [p. 54]

- The school creates a safe, caring environment characterized by interactions between adults and students that convey high expectations, support, and mutual respect. [p. 55]

- The school implements scheduling and student-grouping practices that are flexible, meet each student's needs, and ensure successful academic growth and personal development. [p. 56]

- The school and students' families are partners in fostering the academic, intellectual, social, and emotional success of each student. [p. 57]

- The school coordinates with community agencies in the delivery of social, physical, and mental health services to meet the needs of students and their families. [p. 59]

- The school's instructional practices and organizational policies demonstrate its belief that each student, with work, effort, and support, can achieve at high levels. [p. 65]

- Teachers promote active engagement of each student in his or her own learning through coaching and facilitating. [p. 69]

Equity

Each student must have open and equal access to appropriate and challenging classes and programs as well as the support needed for success. Consider how well your school promotes excellence through equity and access. Access to challenging classes is not enough. Systematically encouraging each student to challenge him- or herself in every lesson and in taking the most advanced courses possible must be the norm in schools. Setting the challenge bar too low for an individual because of preconceived notions is tantamount to lowering expectations for society in general.

Recommendations

- The principal leads in developing, articulating, and committing to a shared vision and mission focused on student success. [p. 42]

- The school provides meaningful decision-making roles for staff members, students, and parents. [p. 43]

- The school values diversity and fosters an array of viewpoints, perspectives, and experiences. [p. 47]

- The school collaboratively develops and reviews with each student a personal plan for progress that promotes ownership of the student's learning goals and provides strategies for achieving high standards. [p. 54]

- The school creates a safe, caring environment characterized by interactions between adults and students that convey high expectations, support, and mutual respect. [p. 55]

- The school implements scheduling and student-grouping practices that are flexible, meet each student's needs, and ensure successful academic growth and personal development. [p. 56]

- The school and students' families are partners in fostering the academic, intellectual, social, and emotional success of each student. [p. 57]

- The school advocates and models a set of core values that are essential in a democratic and civil society. [p. 58]

- The school offers alternatives to tracking and ability grouping while maintaining the flexibility to appropriately support and challenge each student. [p. 61]

- The school's instructional practices and organizational policies demonstrate its belief that each student—with work, effort, and support—can achieve at high levels. [p. 65]

- Teachers promote active engagement of each student in his or her own learning through coaching and facilitating. [p. 69]

Breaking Ranks Framework Recommendations

Core Area: Collaborative Leadership

1. The principal leads in developing, articulating, and committing to a shared vision and mission focused on student success.
2. The school provides meaningful decision-making roles for staff members, students, and parents.
3. All members of the school community actively collaborate to develop and implement the agreed-upon learning goals and improvement plan.
4. Teachers and teacher teams provide the leadership that is essential to student success.
5. Each staff member develops a personal learning plan (PLP) that is aligned with the school improvement plan.
6. The school values diversity and fosters an array of viewpoints, perspectives, and experiences.
7. The school develops partnerships with postsecondary institutions to enhance learning for students and adults.
8. The school develops partnerships with individuals, organizations, community agencies, and businesses to support its mission.
9. The school, in addition to its continual monitoring of progress and yearly reporting, will convene a broad-based panel to conduct an in-depth assessment and present their findings to the public at least once every three years.

Core Area: Personalizing Your School Environment

10. The school establishes structures and practices to banish anonymity and individualize the learning experience for each student.
11. The school reduces the number of students each teacher is responsible for teaching to ensure that each student receives individualized high-quality instruction, feedback, and support.
12. The school collaboratively develops and reviews with each student a personal plan for progress that promotes ownership of the student's learning goals and provides strategies for achieving high standards.
13. The school creates a safe, caring environment characterized by interactions between adults and students that convey high expectations, support, and mutual respect.
14. The school implements scheduling and student-grouping practices that are flexible, meet each student's needs, and ensure successful academic growth and personal development.
15. The school and students' families are partners in fostering the academic, intellectual, social, and emotional success of each student.
16. The school advocates and models a set of core values that are essential in a democratic and civil society.
17. The school coordinates with community agencies in the delivery of social, physical, and mental health services to meet the needs of students and their families.

Core Area: Curriculum, Instruction, and Assessment

18. The school identifies essential learnings and the standards for mastery in all subjects.

19. The school offers alternatives to tracking and ability grouping while maintaining the flexibility to appropriately support and challenge each student.

20. The school fosters collaboration to improve student performance through such structures as teacher teams and regularly scheduled common planning time.

21. The school connects its curriculum to real-life applications and extends learning opportunities beyond its campus.

22. The school supports and extends academic learning and personal development for each student through such structures as service learning, community service, and student activities.

23. The school's instructional practices and organizational policies demonstrate its belief that each student—with work, effort, and support—can achieve at high levels.

24. Teachers plan and deliver challenging, developmentally appropriate lessons that actively engage each student; emphasize depth over breadth; and develop skills, such as creative and critical thinking, problem solving, decision making, and communication.

25. Teachers design and use formative and summative assessments to inform instruction, advance learning, accommodate individual learning needs, and monitor student progress.

26. Each educator possesses pedagogical expertise, a broad academic foundation, in-depth content knowledge in the subjects taught, and an understanding of the developmental needs of his or her students.

27. Teachers promote active engagement of each student in his or her own learning through coaching and facilitating.

28. The school ensures a smooth academic and social transition for each student from grade to grade and school to school.

29. The staff and students use current technology to improve instruction, enhance individualized learning, and facilitate management and operations.

The Complete Picture

As the following figure illustrates, today's school is a complex institution, with many interrelated components. Change one and you will undoubtedly alter another. As outlined in the 29 preceding recommendations, the *Breaking Ranks* Framework addresses the complexity of this institution with specific recommendations for change. The recommendations are based on extensive experience and research and are closely aligned with well-respected work done by other organizations such as the National Middle School Association's *This We Believe: Keys to Educating Young Adolescents* (2010) and the Schools to Watch criteria of the National Forum to Accelerate Middle Grades Reform. (See Appendix 2 for alignment of these initiatives with the *Breaking Ranks* Framework.)

The *Breaking Ranks* Framework, the cornerstones, the core areas, and the recommendations are a lot to digest. The Venn diagram below will help you visualize the many interrelated parts. Alter one and you affect another. Only by breaking things down into discrete components is it possible to reflect on what needs to improve and how. On the following pages, each of the recommendations is provided with a series of strategies, benefits, challenges, and progress measures. As you read, it must be high on your agenda to reflect on how other areas of your school may be affected by possible solutions. The Venn diagram provides a graphic to help your team understand the various connections. Design your improvements to use those connections to your advantage and anticipate reactions and effects—rather than viewing improvement as a single initiative that will only alter one area. Another way to look at the relationship between the cornerstones, the recommendations, and the core areas is presented in the table on the next page.

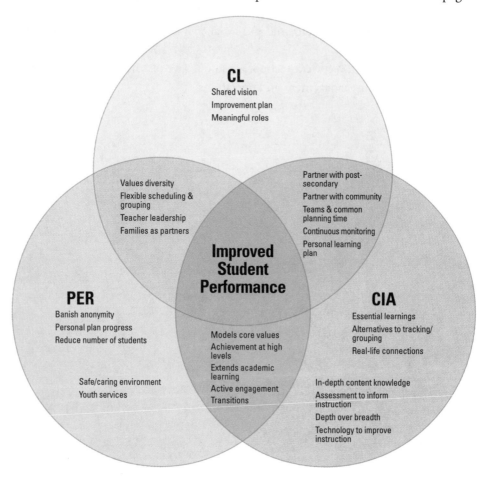

Cornerstones	Core Areas		
	Collaborative Leadership	Personalizing Your School Environment	Curriculum, Instruction, and Assessment
Leadership	<ul><li>shared vision and mission (1)</li><li>meaningful decision-making roles (2)</li><li>collaborates on learning goals and improvement plan (3)</li><li>teachers/teams provide leadership (4)</li><li>personal learning plans for staff (5)</li><li>partnerships with community, etc. (8)</li><li>continuous monitoring (and) in-depth assessment (9)</li></ul>	<ul><li>values diversity and fosters an array of viewpoints (6)</li><li>personal plan for progress for students (12)</li><li>school and students' families are partners (15)</li><li>models core values (16)</li><li>coordinates with community agencies (17)</li></ul>	<ul><li>teacher teams and regularly scheduled common planning time (20)</li><li>active engagement (27)</li><li>smooth academic and social transitions (28)</li></ul>
Professional Development	<ul><li>collaborates on learning goals and improvement plan (3)</li><li>personal learning plans for staff (5)</li><li>school develops partnerships with postsecondary institutions (7)</li></ul>	<ul><li>values diversity and fosters an array of viewpoints (6)</li></ul>	<ul><li>teacher teams and regularly scheduled common planning time (20)</li><li>lessons emphasize depth over breadth (24)</li><li>formative and summative assessment strategies (25)</li><li>pedagogical expertise, in-depth content knowledge (26)</li><li>active engagement (27)</li></ul>
Culture	<ul><li>shared vision and mission (1)</li><li>meaningful decision-making roles (2)</li><li>teachers/teams provide leadership (4)</li></ul>	<ul><li>values diversity and fosters an array of viewpoints (6)</li><li>a safe, caring environment (13)</li><li>school and students' families are partners (15)</li><li>models core values (16)</li></ul>	<ul><li>teacher teams and regularly scheduled common planning time (20)</li><li>each student can achieve at high levels (23)</li><li>active engagement (27)</li></ul>
Organization	<ul><li>collaborates on learning goals and improvement plan (3)</li><li>teachers/teams provide leadership (4)</li></ul>	<ul><li>banishes anonymity and individualizes learning (10)</li><li>reduces the number of students per teacher (11)</li><li>scheduling and student grouping practices are flexible (14)</li></ul>	<ul><li>alternatives to tracking and ability grouping (19)</li><li>teacher teams and regularly scheduled common planning time (20)</li><li>extends academic learning and personal development (22)</li></ul>

Note that some recommendations can be found within multiple cornerstones or core areas. Any initiative can have ripple effects in other areas—and school leaders must understand and plan for the possible connections and reactions to any initiative.

WHAT?

| | Core Areas | | |
Cornerstones	Collaborative Leadership	Personalizing Your School Environment	Curriculum, Instruction, and Assessment
Curriculum	• shared vision and mission (1) • collaborates on learning goals and improvement plan (3) • school develops partnerships with post-secondary institutions (7)	• reduces the number of students per teacher (11) • personal plan for progress for students (12) • models core values (16)	• identifies essential learnings and the standards for mastery (18) • connects its curriculum to real-life applications (21) • extends academic learning and personal development (22) • pedagogical expertise, in-depth content knowledge (26) • smooth academic and social transitions (28)
Instruction	• shared vision and mission (1) • collaborates on learning goals and improvement plan (3)	• reduces the number of students per teacher (11) • scheduling and student grouping practices are flexible (14)	• alternatives to tracking and ability grouping (19) • teacher teams and regularly scheduled common planning time (20) • each student can achieve at high levels (23) • lessons emphasize depth over breadth (24) • pedagogical expertise, in-depth content knowledge (26) • active engagement (27) • use current technology to improve instruction (29)
Assessment	• shared vision and mission (1) • collaborates on learning goals and improvement plan (3)	• reduces the number of students per teacher (11) • scheduling and student grouping practices are flexible (14)	• alternatives to tracking and ability grouping (19) • teacher teams and regularly scheduled common planning time (20) • each student can achieve at high levels (23) • lessons emphasize depth over breadth (24) • formative and summative assessment (25) • pedagogical expertise, in-depth content knowledge (26) • use current technology to improve instruction (29)

WHAT?

Cornerstones	Collaborative Leadership	Personalizing Your School Environment	Curriculum, Instruction, and Assessment
Relationships	• meaningful decision-making roles (2) • collaborates on learning goals and improvement plan (3)	• values diversity and fosters an array of viewpoints (6) • banishes anonymity and individualizes learning (10) • reduces the number of students per teacher (11) • personal plan for progress for students (12) • a safe, caring environment (13) • scheduling and student grouping practices are flexible (14) • school and students' families are partners (15) • coordinates with community agencies (17)	• each student can achieve at high levels (23) • active engagement (27)
Equity	• shared vision and mission (1) • meaningful decision-making roles (2)	• values diversity and fosters an array of viewpoints (6) • personal plan for progress for students (12) • a safe, caring environment (13) • scheduling and student grouping practices are flexible (14) • school and students' families are partners (15) • models core values (16)	• alternatives to tracking and ability grouping (19) • each student can achieve at high levels (23) • active engagement (27)

Note that some recommendations can be found within multiple cornerstones or core areas. Any initiative can have ripple effects in other areas—and school leaders must understand and plan for the possible connections and reactions to any initiative.

WHAT?

COLLABORATIVE LEADERSHIP

WHAT?

RECOMMENDATION 1: **The principal leads in developing, articulating, and committing to a shared vision and mission focused on student success.**

Strategies
- Develop a personal vision of school success that is based on sound educational beliefs that speak to the dignity, equality, and uniqueness of the students served by the school.
- Serve as a collaborative leader who values the voice of stakeholders, cultivates leadership skills in others, and models effective communication.
- Serve as an instructional leader who supports, encourages, and celebrates practices that result in student successes.
- Review and refine the school's vision and mission on a regular basis.
- Use a wide variety of communication tools, such as forums, surveys, newsletters, and Web sites to collect data about student, teacher, and parent satisfaction; identify school strengths and areas for improvement; and keep all stakeholders informed of the school's improvement efforts.
- Ensure the school's vision and mission is in alignment with the district's vision and mission.
- Administer the NASSP 21st Century School Leadership Skills Inventory.
- Identify an experienced mentor and schedule regular time for discussions.
- Build a support network with colleagues.
- Take advantage of resources offered by professional organizations, such as NASSP.
- Model lifelong learning by being a reflective learner, staying abreast of current trends in education, reading professional material, and attending to personal professional development.

Benefits
- Provides the school community with a clearly articulated direction
- Creates shared purpose and trust among all members of the school community as they work as a team to ensure student success
- Develops the leadership skills of the principal and others
- Creates a culture of shared ownership and responsibility for student success
- Places what is best for students at the center of school decision making
- Requires ongoing data-driven evaluation of student progress to ensure the school is advancing its mission

Challenges
- Changing a school's culture, which takes considerable time, effort, and resources
- Balancing the time necessary for purposeful instructional leadership against the demands of operational management
- Needing additional knowledge of diverse student needs, instructional strategies, or content to improve instructional practices in each academic discipline
- Possessing the necessary knowledge, skills, and dispositions to effectively lead sustainable change
- Locating a compatible mentor who has the time, willingness, skills, and commitment to provide coaching and support

Progress Measures
- Collect and analyze data on student, teacher, and parent satisfaction with the school's performance.
- Collect and analyze data on the principal's ability to involve others in the school improvement process.
- Use school and student data from a wide variety of sources to determine the degree to which the vision has been collaboratively developed, clearly articulated, and consistently supported.
- Examine programs, practices, and resource allotment for their impact on student learning and achievement.
- Participate in the NASSP Leadership Skills Inventory.

RECOMMENDATION 2: The school provides meaningful decision-making roles for staff members, students, and parents.

Strategies
- Establish a school leadership team that meets regularly to provide input and guidance to the administration.
- Create a broad-based site council—consisting of administration, teachers, support staff members, parents, community members, and students when appropriate—that is responsible for overseeing school improvement efforts to:
  - Collaboratively determine parameters and authority for decision making
  - Train members in group process and facilitation skills
  - Meet on a regular basis
  - Share minutes/actions with other stakeholders.
- Provide students with opportunities to participate in the school governance through such structures as a principal's advisory council, a leadership club, a student council, etc.
- Use staff meetings for gathering input and making decisions.
- Gather input from members of such parent organizations as PTA or booster clubs.
- Host informational sessions for current and prospective parents and others in the feeder pattern and seek feedback.

Benefits
- Ensures that the voices of the entire school community are heard and valued
- Enlists all segments of the school community to help accomplish schoolwide initiatives
- Builds strong student connections to the school by ensuring their voices are valued
- Creates a learning community in which all stakeholders take ownership of the educational process and are vested in helping to improve learning
- Develops leadership skills that enhance the school's capacity to identify challenges and take appropriate and decisive action
- Promotes sustainable change that endures through changes in leadership

Challenges
- Developing a culture that supports the concept of shared decision making
- Ensuring representation from diverse groups and maintaining interest and enthusiasm over time
- Clarifying and revising existing leadership practices and accountability structures
- Developing the leadership skills necessary to facilitate authentic collaboration among constituencies with divergent agendas
- Ensuring that nonstaff participants believe that their opinions are as valued as those of staff members
- Creating a school culture that respects and supports the voice of students and parents
- Providing non-English-speaking parents and students with meaningful roles in the decision-making process

Progress Measures
- Collect artifacts that document the establishment of a site council and other school advisory groups.
- Communicate the agreed-upon parameters for site council and school advisory groups to all appropriate stakeholders.
- Determine measurable and significant outcomes that have resulted from decisions made by the site council, the leadership team, student groups, advisory councils, and others.
- Conduct surveys or focus groups to determine staff member, parent, student, and community satisfaction with their participation in the decision-making process.
- Collect disaggregated data on the number of participants in the various groups.

COLLABORATIVE LEADERSHIP

WHAT?

RECOMMENDATION 3: All members of the school community actively collaborate to develop and implement the agreed-upon learning goals and improvement plan.

Strategies

- Provide professional development opportunities to cultivate skills in working collaboratively and in creating professional learning communities.
- Use a collaborative process to create the school improvement plan and establish student improvement goals.
- Establish measurable benchmarks and encourage teams to regularly review disaggregated data and use it to guide instruction.
- Create an interdisciplinary school team to coordinate learning goals across departments and teams and for vertical alignment.
- Establish a district or feeder pattern committee to ensure articulation and planning across grade levels and schools.
- Build a school culture that ensures that all staff members seek to be participating members of a common mission.
- Ensure dedicated time for collaboration among and between teams and groups of teachers.
- Create and publish monthly curriculum maps to promote cross-curricular connections.

Benefits

- Establishes realistic learning goals that reflect state and local requirements
- Encourages staff members to take risks, try new instructional strategies, and become more responsive to student needs—all within a supportive learning community
- Promotes staff members' ownership and responsibility for student learning and success
- Supports the school vision and mission by developing a clarity of purpose and a sense of direction
- Fosters an atmosphere of collegiality and respect in which ideas are shared without risk of ridicule
- Provides students with a role-model for mutual respect and cooperation

Challenges

- Focusing strictly on meeting state and district standards, which can narrow the focus of instruction, inhibit creativity and risk taking, and lead to rigidity
- Creating a school culture that requires collaboration and active sharing by all members of the school community, which is sometimes viewed as threatening by the administration and/or staff members
- Ensuring that all staff members, including the principal, possess the skills and resources needed for authentic collaboration

Progress Measures

- Establish and share measurable learning goals and desired student achievement outcomes across teams and departments.
- Review assessment data to document student achievement progress as related to specific instructional strategies.
- Use disaggregated data to identify students who need additional support in specific areas.
- Gather and analyze data that determines the school community's understanding of and commitment to the established learning goals and improvement plan.
- Analyze student attendance, discipline, and achievement data to determine improvements in student achievement, attendance, and behavior.
- Use lesson plans and observations to determine the extent to which the agreed-upon learning goals are being implemented in each classroom.

RECOMMENDATION 4: Teachers and teacher teams provide the leadership that is essential to student success.

Strategies

- Expect teachers returning from a conference, workshop, or other professional development event to share their learning with other staff members.
- Encourage professional development that helps teachers gain expertise in topics and concepts that can be used to improve the instructional practices of all.
- Develop teacher leadership skills in such areas as facilitation, group process, communication, and teaming.
- Encourage teachers to serve as school ambassadors in the community and share with community members how they can support the school's mission and vision to ensure student success.
- Provide opportunities for all teachers to serve in a variety of short- or long-term leadership roles within the school and district.
- Encourage teachers to define their needs, identify problem areas, develop resources and solutions to address the challenges, and share outcomes with their colleagues.
- Work with local teacher associations to develop contract language that promotes teacher leadership.
- Support teachers who are risktakers and want to work in new and creative ways.
- Communicate and support high expectations for each teacher's participation in school improvement work.

Benefits

- Creates effective and sustainable support for school improvement
- Increases support for school improvement work through teacher communication with community members
- Promotes professional development
- Builds and supports a collaborative environment
- Engages teachers as professionals both in and out of the classroom
- Develops the leadership necessary for the school's future successes

Challenges

- Addressing existing leadership structures that impede giving staff members additional authority
- Finding resources and time for authentic collaboration, creation of professional portfolios, and professional development opportunities
- Overcoming established contract language that does not promote teacher leadership and proposing changes and solutions for the future
- Working with teachers and administrators who are reluctant to step into new or redefined leadership roles

Progress Measures

- Measure teacher satisfaction of shared ownership of policies, procedures, and programs through surveys, focus groups, or other methods.
- Document evidence (anecdotal or objective) of increased student engagement or performance resulting from specific strategies learned through collaboration with colleagues.
- Record minutes of team and department meetings.
- Collect data on the number of teachers participating in leadership opportunities.
- Expect teachers to document participation in school improvement work using a portfolio that includes such items as leadership activities, professional development experiences, a log of professional literature read, self-reflections, student data, lesson plans, and student surveys.

COLLABORATIVE LEADERSHIP

WHAT?

COLLABORATIVE LEADERSHIP

WHAT?

RECOMMENDATION 5: Each staff member develops a personal learning plan (PLP) that is aligned with the school improvement plan.

Strategies

- Ensure that the school improvement plan is focused on student success and that all staff members are able to play an active role in its implementation.
- Expect that teachers regularly use self-reflection practices to assess their personal strengths and areas for growth.
- Meet with each staff member to collaboratively assess his or her professional development needs and develop a PLP that is tailored to meet the individual's needs as well as advance the school improvement plan.
- Ensure that each instructional staff member—administrators, teachers, and support staff members—has developed a PLP that advances their individual learning as well as student learning.
- Promote practices that support teachers as adult learners, such as action research, reading and discussing professional literature, peer observation, coaching, and the like.
- Allocate resources and time during school hours to address individual professional development needs.
- Adopt a coaching, goal-setting, or mentoring program in which teachers develop skills needed to meet the goals of their PLP.
- Provide beginning teachers with a mentor for a minimum of two years.
- Encourage all teachers to regularly collaborate with colleagues to increase content knowledge, improve pedagogical practices, and better understand student needs.

Benefits

- Encourages staff members to reflect on their individual strengths and weaknesses and prioritize professional development needs accordingly
- Aligns professional development with the individual needs of teachers and the students they teach
- Identifies the effectiveness of different types of professional development (e.g., seminars, workshops, in-classroom mentoring, peer coaching, and other job-embedded approaches) in meeting school and student learning goals
- Provides educators with opportunities to document their growth as teachers and to coach colleagues on effective strategies for professional growth
- Views instructional support staff members as critical to student success

Challenges

- Establishing professional development as a high priority despite budget constraints and other time demands on staff members
- Motivating staff to address individual professional needs rather than engaging in safe, one-size-fits-all professional development activities
- Addressing union contracts that specify professional development structures
- Changing the perceptions of those who do not view instructional support staff as critical to student success

Progress Measures

- Ensure that each PLP aligns with school improvement goals and includes benchmarks for measurable professional growth as well as a timeline for self-reflection and a plan to gather external feedback.
- Ensure that staff members maintain a portfolio containing evidence of student outcomes as well as documenting personal successes and challenges.
- Schedule at least one mid-year meeting with each staff member to review, revise, and assess progress of the PLP.
- Conduct an annual review of individual and schoolwide professional development activities to determine the impact on advancing the goals of the school improvement plan.

RECOMMENDATION 6: The school values diversity and fosters an array of viewpoints, perspectives, and experiences.

Strategies

- Provide professional development that enables all staff members to see diversity as a benefit to the school by providing a variety of viewpoints, perspectives, experiences, and backgrounds.
- Review curriculum regularly to be sure that it is inclusive and nonbiased.
- Create instructional guides that promote diversity of opinion, expression, and background for each subject and classroom.
- Develop cross-curricular lessons that demonstrate how diversity of opinion is at the heart of our democracy and how those opinions have led to important developments in U.S. and world history.
- Develop staff member and student sensitivity to customs and traditions of others through professional development as well as practices, such as informational nights, culturally relevant newsletters, international festival, student clubs, and so on.
- Differentiate instruction to address diversity in student learning and processing styles and provide students with adult advocates and mentors to build relationships.
- Recruit and hire staff members with diverse backgrounds, viewpoints, perspectives, and experiences.
- Encourage instructional strategies that promote student questioning and opinion sharing.

Benefits

- Exposes students and staff members to viewpoints and perspectives they may not have otherwise considered
- Enriches the learning experience and curriculum by expanding horizons
- Creates a genuine multicultural community in which differences are honored and not viewed as a detriment
- Reinforces the idea that everyone is different, and that each person is valuable and has gifts to share
- Develops an environment that encourages individualism and engages each student in learning, especially those who may have viewed themselves as "different"

Challenges

- Confronting the biases—e.g., racial, ideological, political—of staff members, students, texts, and the community
- Defining diversity to include all variations in human differences
- Locating appropriate materials and the resources to provide professional development
- Translating sensitivity to diversity into respecting and valuing diversity
- Addressing unfair biases toward segments of the population that are created by world affairs

Progress Measures

- Conduct frequent evaluations of curricula and staff development programs as well as classroom, cocurricular, and other school activities to ensure that all promote and value diversity.
- Document changes in disciplinary incidents involving cross-cultural or cross-population violence or bullying.
- Observe classrooms to gather data on student-to-teacher and student-to-student interactions.
- Solicit perceptions on the success of the diversity outreach in the school from representative students.
- Document the effect of the diversity outreach on student achievement, involvement in student activities, the number of students participating in challenging courses, and student plans for the future.

COLLABORATIVE LEADERSHIP

WHAT?

RECOMMENDATION 7: The school develops partnerships with postsecondary institutions to enhance learning for students and adults.

Strategies

- Establish relationships with professors who are willing to share their subject-area expertise with teachers and students.
- Encourage professors to spend sabbatical time as a staff member in your school.
- Promote the exchange of technology and other instructional support materials.
- Communicate upcoming events, lectures, and projects that might be of interest to teachers, students, professors, and preservice teachers.
- Use undergraduates to assist in classrooms.
- Invite professors to attend professional development offerings at your school.
- Build strong relationships with local schools of education through the placement of preservice teachers in the school, coteaching classes with college personnel, and inviting professors to provide professional development to your staff members in their areas of expertise.
- Invite postsecondary educators to shadow teachers and students to gain a perspective of life in today's schools.
- Engage in open dialogue with postsecondary institutions regarding how your school can better address preparing students for postsecondary success.
- Engage in joint efforts to align preK–16 curriculum and goals.
- Work with your postsecondary partner to develop school-based master's programs or summer institutes in school improvement and other instructional areas.
- Establish dual-enrollment programs that allow high school students to gain college credit prior to graduation.

Benefits

- Provides the school with educational experts and researchers to help teachers enhance their skills and take advantage of current practices of teaching and learning
- Helps translate abstract research into practice
- Increases the responsiveness and currency of postsecondary offerings
- Improves teacher retention, especially for beginning teachers, by providing additional support and advice
- Reinforces the idea that everyone in a learning community should be a lifelong learner
- Exposes students to the benefits of postsecondary education at an early age
- Improves articulation of preK–16 curriculum and learning goals across all levels
- Provides the school with access to the latest research, recommendations of current books for staff discussion, and resources for action research
- Gives the school the opportunity to preview and hire high-quality personnel from teacher- and administrator-preparation programs
- Provides opportunities for the school and the postsecondary institution to seek and obtain grants for joint studies and other initiatives

Challenges

- Creating partnerships between schools and postsecondary institutions that are geographically distant
- Finding the time, money, and energy to coordinate programs
- Establishing a formal partnership with defined roles and benefits for all participants

Progress Measures

- Determine desired outcomes for the partnership(s) and evaluate the satisfaction level of those participating in the partnership.
- Track the number of students who participate in dual-enrollment programs, classes that visit the campus of postsecondary institutions, classroom presentations given by faculty of postsecondary institutions, and so on.
- Document the benefits to the school and to the postsecondary institution, such as the number of practicum and student teachers trained at the school, graduates hired by the school, school educators who participated in classes or other professional development opportunities, visits to classrooms by postsecondary faculty for research, and the like.

RECOMMENDATION 8: The school develops partnerships with individuals, organizations, community agencies, and businesses to support its mission.

Strategies

- Assess the needs of the school to determine what type of outside assistance and support is required to advance the school's mission.
- Use the NASSP How-To Guide for School/Business Partnership to aid in the creation of formal partnerships (www.nassp.org/businesspartnerships).
- Establish a community advisory board composed of parents, service organizations, and local business representatives to assess and access community resources and opportunities that will help further the school's mission.
- Enlist the involvement of local businesses, community groups, retired businesspeople, and others in advancing the school's mission by collaborating on projects; establishing a volunteer program; and providing internships, mentorships, tutoring programs, shadowing experiences, and other opportunities for students to learn outside the walls of the school.
- Maintain an open-door policy that encourages parents and community members to visit and volunteer at the school.
- Develop and clearly articulate a public engagement strategy that calls upon all staff members to participate.
- Develop a list of key community and business leaders in your area and include citizens known to be well-informed and respected. Contact them personally and introduce yourself as someone they can call if they have questions about the education programs in your area. Put them on the mailing list for your newsletter. Invite them to concerts, sporting events, open houses, and other programs at your school.
- Host a breakfast for the realtors in your area, give them a tour of the school, and let students share stories of success with them.
- Stay in contact with your state representatives, invite them to visit your school to speak with students when they are not in session.
- Create service-learning projects that link core standards to global issues and include opportunities to bring in community members to speak to and work with students.
- Know your state's legislative schedule and structure so that you can contact key people at the most opportune times.

Benefits

- Provides community members with a firsthand look at the school and allows them to develop a supportive, trusting relationship with the school
- Creates stronger relationships between the school and the community it serves
- Opens opportunities for a variety of needed resources, such as financial, programmatic, volunteer, talent, social services, and moral support

Challenges

- Helping community members understand the goals and mission of the school, how they can support that mission, and how the relationships can be mutually beneficial
- Providing the needed time and resources to coordinate these efforts
- Gaining firm commitments from others and ensuring that their time is not wasted
- Ensuring that funds raised through local businesses are used wisely so that the relationship continues
- Ensuring that partnership support does not overly influence educational decision making
- Encouraging participation by diverse segments of the community, rather than only those who are traditionally involved

Progress Measures

- Collect and analyze data regularly to determine the accomplishments, strengths, and weaknesses of the various partnerships.
- Determine how well efforts address the stated needs of the school and students.
- Track number of volunteer hours, financial resources, and other benefits provided to the school by the partnership.
- Predetermined mutually agreed-upon benchmarks and expectations for partnership success; regularly assess progress, both formally and informally.
- Document benefits to be derived by parties involved in each partnership and review on an annual basis.

COLLABORATIVE LEADERSHIP

WHAT?

COLLABORATIVE LEADERSHIP

WHAT?

RECOMMENDATION 9: The school, in addition to its continual monitoring of progress and yearly reporting, will convene a broad-based panel to conduct an in-depth assessment and present their findings to the public at least once every three years.

Strategies

- Ensure the leadership team and the site council collect and analyze data on a regular basis to determine progress toward the school improvement goals.
- Provide regular, clear communication to the school community on progress toward meeting student learning and school improvement goals.
- Conduct and publish the results of an in-depth review of school policies, procedures, practices and progress at least once every three years by such processes as:
  - Creating a review council consisting of school personnel and business community members, higher education partners, parents, community groups, or others to conduct the review
  - Participating in a formal national, state, or regional accreditation process
  - Competing in a national, state, or regional school recognition program that requires a thorough review of school policies, practices, programs, and progress in meeting student needs
  - Hiring an outside evaluation firm to review the school and provide the report.

Benefits

- Requires that data be examined on a regular basis to determine progress toward goals
- Demonstrates an openness for constructive criticism and emphasizes that the school has nothing to hide
- Provides the community with a clear picture of the school's achievements and successes and explains how challenges to improve student performance are being addressed
- Provides independent confirmation to prospective and current parents, the community, and educators that the school's academic program is rigorous and the learning environment is healthy for each student
- Provides the school with an unbiased look at its performance that can be used to clarify and focus future improvement efforts
- Enhances the school's improvement efforts and allows outside experts to see the school's needs firsthand

Challenges

- Building continual progress monitoring into the process of school improvement
- Ensuring that the three-year review is based on broad, unbiased participation so that the report is honest and accurate and not a reflection of what the school wishes to project as the school's image
- Responding to school and community concerns when goals are not met or a report is not favorable to the school
- Creating a panel that is knowledgeable and unbiased

Progress Measures

- Gather and analyze data to determine progress toward school improvement goals.
- Document the process used to conduct the three-year review—who participated, how input was solicited, what data were used, what outcomes were reported, and how information was shared with the school community.
- Demonstrate how information gathered from the yearly and the three-year reports have been incorporated into determining goals for school improvement.

RECOMMENDATION 10: The school establishes structures and practices to banish anonymity and individualize the learning experience for each student.

Strategies

- Organize the school into smaller units, such as interdisciplinary teams, schools-within-a-school, or small learning communities.
- Ensure that the smaller units reflect the diversity of the school population, including students with special needs.
- Use looping or multiage grouping so that students and adults have opportunities to build long-term relationships.
- Provide professional development for teachers about heterogeneous grouping and the benefits of differentiating lessons.
- Use instructional strategies that encourage small groups or pairs of students to work together for extended periods in all classes.
- Include all staff members in the small units so that every adult in the school has a role in ensuring that each student is known and understood.
- Provide professional development to ensure that staff members are successful in their efforts to guarantee that all students are known, understood, and cared for.
- Celebrate publicly the successes of small units in ensuring that their student members are known, understood, and cared for.
- Ensure that each student has an adult advocate.
- Establish a schoolwide advisory program for all students:
  - Assign a group of students to an adult who will serve as their adviser and advocate
  - Develop goals, curricula, and outcomes for the program to support each student's academic success and personal development
  - Provide staff members with the professional development necessary to be an effective adviser and mentor to students
  - Schedule regular meeting times to allow for student-staff relationships to grow.

Benefits

- Creates a support network for each student
- Fosters the recognition of each student by adults in the school
- Creates a caring structure to monitor each student's progress
- Teaches each student necessary skills to advocate for him- or herself
- Enables the school to more effectively appropriate resources to meet each student's needs
- Promotes student self-discipline through high expectations
- Improves school climate
- Diminishes alienation among students and promotes individual responsibility
- Builds relationships between students and adults that reduce the bias and prejudice that lead to bullying
- Allows each student to be known, understood, and recognized for his or her talents, not isolated because of disabilities, language differences, or culture
- Teaches students to learn how to work together on intellectual tasks
- Ensures that every student in the school knows and is known by an adult
- Helps adults acquire a better understanding for what is going on in the lives of students
- Decreases disciplinary problems by giving each student a sense of worth and a genuine connection to a caring adult
- Provides students with an adult to turn to in times of need
- Increases opportunities for students to receive extra help
- Creates a more-personalized learning community
- Increases student engagement leading to academic gains for all

(continued)

PERSONALIZING YOUR SCHOOL ENVIRONMENT

WHAT?

RECOMMENDATION 10 *(continued)*

Challenges

- Growing student enrollment, overcrowding, and budget cutbacks
- Overcoming parental objections
- Training staff to take on new roles
- Overcoming the perception that English language learners and students with special needs must be isolated to protect them
- Overcoming preconceived negative attitudes of some staff members regarding activities that require them to go beyond their role of only teaching their subject
- Overcoming the reluctance of leaders in the school to participate and model behaviors that ensure that each student is known, understood, and cared for
- Scheduling a consistent time for advisories to meet while addressing other demands on staff members' time
- Finding additional resources to recruit and train outside mentors
- Making sure that each child has an advocate who takes the assignment seriously and makes it meaningful for the student
- Addressing the reluctance of some adults to face difficult personal issues encountered by students
- Providing staff members with training on strategies to help students with personal issues

Progress Measures

- Establish structures to collect data on the progress of each smaller unit in ensuring that all its student members are known, understood, and cared for.
- Monitor team, advisory, and SLC membership to ensure that their composition reflects the diversity of the school population including English language learners and students with special needs.
- Document improved student achievement and behavior by regularly analyzing disciplinary records and test results.
- Establish practices and structures to confirm that each student is known, understood, and cared for by a trusted adult.
- Measure the degree to which the advisory program includes every student, develops relationships between advisers and advisees, and offers adequate time to build relationships.
- Review student achievement and disciplinary data in light of this program.
- Document teacher contacts with the students for whom they are responsible through logs kept by each adviser.
- Conduct periodic, random checks with students by counselors to verify positive relationships with their advisers.

RECOMMENDATION 11: The school reduces the number of students each teacher is responsible for teaching to ensure that each student receives individualized high-quality instruction, feedback, and support.

Strategies

- Create teams of students and teachers with no more than 90 students on a team. Schedule as close as possible to a maximum ratio of 90:1 for core-area teachers.
- Prioritize staffing allocations among all positions to increase the number of teachers and reduce the student-to-teacher ratio.
- Consolidate nonteaching school positions to hire more teachers.
- Seek outside funding for additional teachers.
- Encourage teachers to define their roles to include the modification of curriculum and instruction on the basis of learner needs and the development of necessary skills.
- Explore alternative scheduling strategies across the course of the school year, semester, quarter, and day.
- Track student achievement in classrooms as it relates to high-quality instruction.
- Gather research done on the topic of student-to-teacher ratio as it directly relates to improved student achievement, critical thinking, and problem-solving skills and share it with decisionmakers.

Benefits

- Gives teachers time and energy to develop nurturing relationships with students and enhances individualized instruction
- Creates a personalized learning environment
- Provides teachers and teacher teams additional time to review student work, monitor individual students, plan and deliver specific performance feedback, plan adaptations for individual students, and collaborate with other teachers to differentiate lessons and better meet specific students' needs
- Helps to ensure that no student's needs are neglected

Challenges

- Addressing difficult choices on program offerings that require cuts in programs that are important but less essential than others
- Creating or finding necessary space, because more classrooms or creative scheduling may be needed
- Identifying methods of reducing ratios without additional money

Progress Measures

- Continually monitor individual and team enrollments to ensure their stability and balance with no more than the agreed-upon minimum.
- Gather data to track the extent to which achievement improves with a reduced student-to-teacher ratio.
- Gather and report data to track the extent to which disciplinary referrals increase or decrease with a reduced student-to-teacher ratio.
- Document the consolidation of nonteaching school positions in an effort to hire more teachers to support increasing the size of nonacademic classes to reduce the student-to-teacher ratio for core-area classes.
- Document the search for outside funding for additional teachers to support increasing the size of nonacademic classes to reduce the student-to-teacher ratio for core-area classes.

PERSONALIZING YOUR SCHOOL ENVIRONMENT

WHAT?

PERSONALIZING YOUR SCHOOL ENVIRONMENT

WHAT?

RECOMMENDATION 12: The school collaboratively develops and reviews with each student a personal plan for progress (PPP) that promotes ownership of the student's learning goals and provides strategies for achieving high standards.

Strategies

- Establish a structure, such as an advisory, that allows advisers to collaborate with students to create and review PPPs that address the academic, social, and developmental needs of each student.
- Assign each teacher to a group of students to monitor and adapt their PPPs to better meet the academic, social, and developmental needs of each.
- Collaborate with each student to present the contents of the PPP to his or her parents in student-led conferences.
- Precede the PPP development process with activities to help students articulate who they are—their skills, interests, passions, history, and experiences.
- Use data from a variety of assessments (e.g., interest, learning style, and intelligence preference) to inform the development of each student's PPP.
- Define student engagement criteria and prepare an observation sheet for recording behaviors in class.

Benefits

- Increases student engagement as students take responsibility for their own learning
- Increases potential for improvement in achievement
- Provides additional opportunities for families to come into the school and actively participate in their children's education
- Fosters student ownership of learning and how to be an advocate for their own learning—which is an asset to the teacher and students
- Gives the teacher and the student a common goal for developing a partnership for learning

Challenges

- Providing time, resources, and training for staff to collaborate with students to plan and review the PPP
- Developing a variety of means for appropriately assessing student progress
- Resisting the temptation to track students so that teachers work with groups of students with similar PPPs
- Creating PPPs that inform meaningful classroom practice
- Creating the PPP process so that it is not an impediment (unproductive paperwork or meetings)
- Ensuring that a student's PPP complements his or her IEP

Progress Measures

- Establish a structure through which each student maintains a secure location a portfolio that contains an up-to-date PPP, a record of implementation steps, examples of the student's work that support and track student performance gains over time, and assessment data.
- Observe and document the degree of increased student engagement in individual learning.
- Collect data to evaluate the effectiveness of the PPP process by reviewing each PPP portfolio; student performance data (including engagement); and the satisfaction level of teachers, students, parents, and other personnel with the PPP process.
- Collect data regarding student and family confidence in the process, the increased capacity of students to plot their own paths, and their understanding of options for the future.

RECOMMENDATION 13: The school creates a safe, caring environment characterized by interactions between adults and students that convey high expectations, support, and mutual respect.

Strategies

- Engage in teaming to foster teacher discussion of students' needs, progress, and plans.
- Foster dignity by developing student's capacity for self-discipline.
- Include strategies for developing relationship-building skills, a more personalized school culture, and habits of practice that convey caring and support.
- Use data gathered from smaller unit teams and advisories to identify individual students in need of additional or specialized support.
- Allocate time to develop strategies to assist students in developing responsible relationships with others.
- Develop, maintain, and broadly communicate an operational plan for ensuring the safety and security of the school community.
- Create a classroom environment in which each student is able to take risks in his or her learning.
- Develop a plan in each classroom for students to contact their mentors or advisers when needed.
- Develop individualized student goals for academics and behavior and have students self-monitor their progress.
- Define classroom expectations with input from students at the beginning of the course, the semester, and the year and regularly update.
- Develop individualized student goals for academics and behavior and have each student monitor their own progress.
- Ensure that adults in the building have a clear understanding of the social and emotional needs of the students they are working with.
- Develop a schoolwide behavioral program that teaches and supports positive student behavior.
- Ensure consistency of expectations from classroom to classroom (e.g., behavior, grading, homework, and so on).

Benefits

- Increases student feeling of being valued, which encourages students to take more responsibility for their learning
- Increases personal responsibility as a classroom citizen and deters discipline problems
- Supports emotional and intellectual development in students
- Fills a void for some students
- Provides a safe haven for students
- Fosters trust
- Develops students' understanding of how to set personal goals

Challenges

- Developing a school culture in which people are expected to care for one another
- Ensuring that professional boundaries are understood by all because caring can be misinterpreted
- Allocating resources and time
- Moving from adult-centered to student-centered environments
- Helping adults accept that all students can achieve at a high level
- Providing training to staff members on how to appropriately differentiate lessons without decreasing their expectations of students

Progress Measures

- Conduct climate surveys of students, staff members, and parents.
- Analyze attendance data for patterns of nonattendance.
- Document and share staff practices of personalization that promote a sense of caring.
- Analyze discipline data to determine changes in student behavior.
- Analyze discipline data by teacher, location, time of day, and so on to determine areas of concern.

PERSONALIZING YOUR SCHOOL ENVIRONMENT

WHAT?

PERSONALIZING YOUR SCHOOL ENVIRONMENT

WHAT?

RECOMMENDATION 14: The school implements scheduling and student-grouping practices that are flexible, meet each student's needs, and ensure successful academic growth and personal development.

Strategies

- Adjust the length of class periods to provide extended periods of time for core classes.
- Consolidate noncore subjects to fewer days per week.
- Adjust the length of the school day; schedule extended days periodically.
- Dedicate a designated number of weeks as concentrated core curriculum weeks.
- Adjust the length of the school year: go to a trimester or year-round school schedule.
- Explore scheduling strategies used by other schools and their results.
- To offer electives and core courses, schedule a period of instruction before the school day begins and after it ends that is staffed by teachers on a flexible schedule.
- Reduce the amount of passing time between classes.

Benefits

- Provides more time devoted to instruction
- Increases the opportunity for project-based instruction
- Creates more time for in-depth work that leads to greater student understanding of key concepts
- Offers flexibility for teacher teams to collaborate for increased student success
- Helps teachers to spend more time on instruction
- Ensures that teacher teams have the flexibility to allot more time to certain classes when necessary without blocks of time being dictated by the master schedule

Challenges

- Deciding on program offerings
- Handling issues related to teacher autonomy and scheduling
- Providing the necessary professional development for teachers to maximize the benefits of new time configurations
- Scheduling common planning time for teams
- Addressing transportation needs, athletic schedules, and other cocurricular schedules

Progress Measures

- Document the impact of flexible scheduling, lengthened class periods, weeks dedicated to core curricula, common planning for teaching teams, and adjusted length of school day and/or year on students' academic growth and personal development.
- Show evidence that teacher teams are engaging in common planning time on a consistent basis (e.g., meeting minutes, reports, team planning products).
- Document changes in the quality of instruction.
- Survey students, parents, and staff members on changes in meeting students' needs.

RECOMMENDATION 15: The school and students' families are partners in fostering the academic, intellectual, social, and emotional success of each student.

Strategies

- Communicate regularly with students' families about their progress through calls, e-mail, or notes from advisers.
- Include parents in development and review of their child's personal plan for progress using student-led conferences held in the school.
- Schedule school events during a variety of hours (e.g., evenings, weekends) to maximize family participation.
- Consider holding school events in the neighborhoods of the families to reduce transportation issues.
- Include information in the school newsletter about school and community resources available to families.
- Create a parent Listserv or other online group to encourage communication with and among parents.
- Develop talents and skills data base for family members and cross-reference it with a list of school needs to aid in recruiting volunteers.
- Expand understanding of family to include nontraditional family structures that exist in your school community and consistently use terminology that demonstrates that understanding.

Benefits

- Helps schools acquire additional resources to support student success
- Involves parents and families in the education of their children and in the school
- Increases academic support for students during the time they are not in school
- Modify standard family contact procedures to communicate with and involve hard-to-contact families

Challenges

- Addressing students' interest in keeping family members away from school involvement
- Overtime or trade-offs for staff members to meet staffing requirements
- Getting family members to respond
- Engaging families who may be afraid to participate because of their immigration status
- Providing translation services

Progress Measures

- Document increased family contacts and participation in decisions about their child's school experiences.
- Document the results of modifications to standard family contact procedures to communicate with and involve hard-to-contact families.
- Record and compare the number of families attending school events and of family volunteers who are active in the school community after strategies to increase contact have been implemented.
- Use a climate and culture survey to examine changes in mutual respect between the families and the school staff.

PERSONALIZING YOUR SCHOOL ENVIRONMENT

WHAT?

PERSONALIZING YOUR SCHOOL ENVIRONMENT

WHAT?

RECOMMENDATION 16: The school advocates and models a set of core values that are essential in a democratic and civil society.

Strategies

- Establish structures and processes through which students participate in decision making about policies and practices related to school culture and operation.
- Create such structures as a peer mediation program to involve students in fair and creative conflict resolution.
- Involve students and staff members in establishing expectations for student and staff conduct and the consequences for noncompliance.
- Involve students in community-based projects and service learning projects.
- Provide opportunities for students to develop skills in decision making, critical thinking, and communication through advisory lessons, developmental guidance groups, and classroom activities.

Benefits

- Develops students' understanding of citizenship values and responsibilities
- Improves the learning climate, which encourages greater student achievement
- Fosters relationship building among students and between students and staff members

Challenges

- Getting student and staff member "buy-in"; creating a climate in which expectations apply to all
- Inspiring teachers to think of community-based or service learning projects to incorporate in their curricula
- Extending school values to the community and students' homes
- Answering skeptics who don't believe that schools should be teaching values

Progress Measures

- Document evidence of student and staff member engagement in formulating school vision, mission, and goals.
- Review data to determine the effectiveness of student mediation.
- Show evidence of an increased number of students participating in activities that raise student voice and participation and in community-involvement activities.

RECOMMENDATION 17: The school coordinates with community agencies in the delivery of social, physical, and mental health services to meet the needs of students and their families.

Strategies
- Create and maintain a resource list of support agencies for use by all school staff members.
- Ensure that all staff members know how to appropriately refer students to community agencies for assistance.
- Establish relationships with community agencies.
- Invite community agencies to deliver programs that encourage students to take advantage of all health and social services available.
- Invite community agencies to deliver their services to students and families on campus.

Benefits
- Involves the community in the school
- Supports teacher efforts to help students by providing links to professionals in health and social services
- Decreases distractions from learning for students who might otherwise be preoccupied with health and other social needs
- Enhances the school's climate of caring for student well-being
- Improves attendance and may prevent students from dropping out
- Helps families with heavy work schedules meet their needs more efficiently

Challenges
- Developing a plan regarding confidentiality issues and permission and consent from families
- Addressing language and cultural issues
- Being sensitive to the social stigma attached to some types of services
- Budgeting for increased costs for additional personnel and extended hours to build the operation
- Dedicating staff members to develop and maintain partnerships

Progress Measures
- Use the results of a climate survey to ascertain the degree of a sense of well-being among the students.
- Identify students with needs and concerns that may be addressed by community agencies, provide increased services for those students, and monitor their absenteeism and performance over the school year.
- Track student attendance, reporting statistics each quarter.

PERSONALIZING YOUR SCHOOL ENVIRONMENT

WHAT?

RECOMMENDATION 18: The school identifies essential learnings and the standards for mastery in all subjects.

Strategies

- Align all schools within attendance patterns to establish a logical continuum of essential learnings (vertical alignment from kindergarten through high school).
- Align course work and instruction with local, state, and national standards.
- Establish habits and standards of learning through extended conversations about the purpose of the school so that the school can develop rigorous standards against which student achievement can be assessed in multiple ways (e.g., testing, portfolios, and projects).
- Integrate discipline-specific staff members into team structures to foster interdisciplinary planning and teaching that allows for the essential learnings to be taught across disciplines and through interdisciplinary projects.
- Establish practices that showcase student-led analysis and discussion of their mastery of essential learnings.
- Define learning goals. Set clear expectations. Assess and revise goals as needed.
- Provide professional development to help staff members create and articulate essential learnings and measure achievement against those goals.
- Set specific readiness targets at each grade level for math and reading proficiency and ensure that they are aligned with college readiness and the common core standards.
- Align grading practices with expectations regarding standards and mastery.

Benefits

- Establishes a focus for student learning and allows students to see their own progress on a path with a logically designed destination and clear expectations
- Aligns course content and practices vertically (K–12), as well as with local, state, and national standards
- Increases student achievement in core subjects and establishes a strong foundation in literacy skills
- Creates the framework for a richer, more meaningful learning experience
- Emphasizes skills and content important to students with special needs

Challenges

- Moving away from course-based instruction and expectations
- Determining the proper level of understanding for a student to advance to the next level
- Aligning essential learnings across schools in the attendance pattern with state and district standards
- Getting student and teacher buy-in
- Addressing language barriers faced by English language learners
- Providing challenges for students who are ready to move to the next level

Progress Measures

- Conduct frequent reviews of student transcripts and permanent records to ensure that every student has access to high-quality learning experiences.
- Identify essential learnings before teaching each course or unit; devise and implement a method by which students can demonstrate what they have learned in a concrete fashion.
- Gather evidence that course work and assessments are aligned vertically (K–12) across the schools in the attendance pattern and with state and national standards.
- Publish math and literacy targets for each grade level.

RECOMMENDATION 19: The school offers alternatives to tracking and ability grouping while maintaining the flexibility to appropriately support and challenge each student.

Strategies
- Provide professional development and support to teachers as they focus on differentiating instruction.
- Use heterogeneous grouping that incorporates English language learners and special education populations at the school, grade, and class levels as appropriate.
- Consider use of multiage classes.
- Create interdisciplinary teams and provide opportunities for cross-discipline connections.
- Provide structured, tiered interventions that can be assessed and measured.
- Provide time for remediation, enrichment, and support.
- Create a mechanism to combat parent misperceptions about ability grouping.
- Provide systems for teachers to support one another.
- Create teams of teachers who decide upon course content, develop syllabi, create common formative and summative assessments, review data, develop a review process, and target remediation efforts.
- Provide additional instructional time to those students in need. Hold standards constant and make time the variable.
- Consider multiyear looping of students and teachers as appropriate.

Benefits
- Ensures equity for all students
- Provides opportunity for peer-to-peer mentoring, character development, and decreased isolation from other students
- Offers rich curricula available to all students
- Creates the opportunity for all students to learn with a diverse group of peers
- Emphasizes tolerance and sensitivity to diversity
- Increases expectations for each student, including English language learners and students with special needs
- Reduces achievement gaps between groups
- Models real-world working environments as students work in collaborative flexible groups

Challenges
- Providing substantial professional development on differentiated instruction
- Keeping more advanced students engaged and motivated
- Addressing parent and staff member perceptions about heterogeneous grouping
- Keeping the academic challenge for each student on an even playing field
- Engaging diverse students in high-level activities

Progress Measures
- Examine longitudinal data for evidence of increased achievement in assessments across all student groups.
- Review grouping and scheduling practices to ensure diversity of economic, ethnic, and achievement groups in all classes.
- Track student performance in mixed-ability groups.
- Document all remediation and enrichment activities, such as students served, time allotted, and topics covered.

CURRICULUM, INSTRUCTION, AND ASSESSMENT

WHAT?

RECOMMENDATION 20: The school fosters collaboration to improve student performance through such structures as teacher teams and regularly scheduled common planning time.

Strategies

- Create teams of teachers who decide on course content, develop syllabi, create common formative and summative assessments, review data, develop a review process, and target remediation efforts.
- Use interdisciplinary teaming where appropriate.
- Create team-based integrated units.
- Promote the integration of literacy across content areas through a literacy council or cross-functional team.
- Identify and examine those skills that are necessary across content areas and determine common benchmarks and strategies to use across the disciplines.
- Create student teams and keep them together as it benefits their instruction.

Benefits

- Encourages students to form relationships with team teachers
- Allows students to see the connections among disciplines
- Creates teams of teachers that take ownership of a specific group of students
- Encourages collaboration and opportunities for teams of teachers to look at student work and talk about individual students in need of assistance
- Allows subjects to be addressed in greater depth

Challenges

- Organizing content across departments
- Aligning with district curriculum and pacing guides
- Providing funding to support new structures
- Soliciting buy-in from teachers
- Seeking agreement on what units to address
- Ensuring teacher and material continuity
- Providing specific, targeted, job-embedded professional development
- Ensuring that curriculum integration is authentic

Progress Measures

- Examine team configuration to ensure that all teachers and students are placed on teams.
- Monitor the process, procedures, and structures created by each team to ensure that literacy, basic skills, common benchmarks, and strategies are taught or used across content areas.

RECOMMENDATION 21: The school connects its curriculum to real-life applications and extends learning opportunities beyond its campus.

Strategies

- Create internships.
- Provide opportunities for community service and service learning.
- Ensure that all high school level career and technical education courses include certification, a work component, and a partnership with a community organization or business.
- Use a variety of methods—such as integrated course work, project-based learning, guest speakers, service learning, exhibitions to the community, student-led conferences, and field trips—to help students make real-life connections between school and the larger world.
- Get to know the students so that their histories, knowledge, and experiences inform staff members and lead to personalized instruction and an understanding of any specific learning gaps.
- Use authentic learning activities, such as having students write a letter to the editor for publication, participate in running a mock business, plan a family vacation or day trip, or participate in simulations.

Benefits

- Provides authentic learning and developmentally appropriate activities for students, regardless of their ages, to try out adult roles
- Demonstrates the connection between the real world and what is taught and learned in the classroom
- Engages students in learning, which leads to increased achievement
- Increases attendance and engagement, which leads to a decrease in disciplinary issues

Challenges

- Allocating time and resources to planning and implementation
- Providing a rigorous academic focus to experiential learning activities
- Aligning learning projects with state curriculum

Progress Measures

- Document each lesson, unit, or segment of learning through the use of highly specific rubrics and student portfolios, the completion of assignments, quality work, and a variety of real-world projects.
- Make public the results and impact of learning as it is applies to school or community issues through team and student presentations.

CURRICULUM, INSTRUCTION, AND ASSESSMENT

WHAT?

CURRICULUM, INSTRUCTION, AND ASSESSMENT

WHAT?

RECOMMENDATION 22: The school supports and extends academic learning and personal development for each student through such structures as service learning, community service, and student activities.

Strategies

- Form partnerships with local community groups to connect students with opportunities that are available in the community.
- Provide teachers with professional development about how to embed service learning into the curriculum.
- Require hours of community service for graduation.
- Ensure that all career and technical education courses include certification, a work component, and a partnership with a community organization or business.
- Provide career- and technical-related introductory activities or courses to students at the middle and elementary levels.
- Ensure that activities and service programs are tied to the courses and goals of the school.
- Define educational objectives and determine criteria for assessment.
- Evaluate all activities, including athletics, in terms of the support they provide for your school's broader learning objectives.
- Create service learning projects that link core standards to global issues and include opportunities to bring in community members to speak to and work with students.
- Offer a wide array of clubs, sports, after-school activities, lunchtime programs, and the like according to student needs and interests.

Benefits

- Increases opportunities for learning and allows students to become engaged in the community, which may lead to fewer discipline problems and increased student achievement
- Provides a potential hook to interest and involve students in school through cocurricular or athletic programs
- Encourages students to see the connections among service programs, student activities, and class work

Challenges

- Providing time, resources, coordination of activities, and transportation and safety for students
- Developing contacts in the community
- Coordinating with independent operating groups
- Identifying age-appropriate activities K–12
- Aligning student activities with the curriculum

Progress Measures

- Determine the number or percentage of students engaged in student activities, and set targets for growth each year.
- Review data on the individual students who are involved in student activities to look for correlations with decreases in discipline problems and increases in student achievement.
- Solicit specific feedback about the quality of the activity through a survey or questionnaire from those participating in service learning, community service, and student activities.

RECOMMENDATION 23: The school's instructional practices and organizational policies demonstrate its belief that each student—with work, effort, and support—can achieve at high levels.

Strategies

- Establish nonnegotiable scope and sequence that are aligned with standards and assessment.
- Provide professional development for teachers that is related to providing high-level instruction for all students.
- Provide resources to help staff members shift their perceptions and practices from a focus on teaching to a focus on learning.
- Develop curriculum units that begin with personal meaning for and experiences of students and end with a celebration and a sense of possibilities for what students can do with this learning.
- Use programs and materials designed to engage students.
- Give teachers released time to develop new programs or adapt existing ones.
- Pair teachers who demonstrate understanding of this recommendation with new teachers and those who need assistance.
- Encourage and support teamwork among teachers.
- Institute standards-based and mastery learning and grading practices.
- Use actual community problems and issues to construct hands-on activities that articulate and demonstrate state and national standards and engage students in the discovery process.
- Adopt cooperative learning activities, peer-to-peer mentoring, project-based learning, use of rubrics, weekly work, and plans.
- Provide staff development for all teachers on language development and cultural and disability issues.
- Provide opportunities for students with special needs to demonstrate mastery in a variety of ways, depending on their readiness, interest, and learning profiles.
- Differentiate instruction regularly.

Benefits

- Helps teachers understand the concepts and importance of engagement
- Provides real-life learning opportunities to students
- Matches instruction to student's developmental needs
- Organizes school around student, not adult, needs
- Creates high expectations and goals for students
- Helps students develop a global understanding of concepts taught in school and their relevance to the real world
- Creates an accepting and nurturing environment for students with disabilities
- Provides mentoring and leadership opportunities for teachers

Challenges

- Addressing a climate of low expectations, particularly for minority students and students with special needs
- Providing the necessary professional development
- Identifying and paying for high-quality programs
- Getting teacher buy-in for new strategies
- Maintaining a qualified and certified workforce

Progress Measures

- Conduct classroom observations of student engagement, time on task, and task persistence.
- Review student work for evidence of critical thinking and problem-solving skills.
- Provide evidence of an increase in student engagement (observation), a decrease in disciplinary issues (review of disciplinary data), and an increase in teacher satisfaction (climate survey) and retention.

CURRICULUM, INSTRUCTION, AND ASSESSMENT

WHAT?

CURRICULUM, INSTRUCTION, AND ASSESSMENT

WHAT?

RECOMMENDATION 24: Teachers plan and deliver challenging, developmentally appropriate lessons that actively engage each student; emphasize depth over breadth; and develop skills, such as creative and critical thinking, problem solving, decision making, and communication.

Strategies

- Identify essential learnings and align curriculum and instruction and instructional time to them.
- Provide in-depth and ongoing professional development on accommodating different learning needs.
- Hire master teachers to work with staff members on new skills.
- Provide time and support for peer observation and feedback so teachers can learn from one another.
- Provide opportunities for students and teachers to assess what learning modalities best suit each learner.
- Provide time for reflection and for integration of English language learners, special education and gifted and talented students, and others.
- Use teachers with special skills in such areas as differentiation, literacy, and inclusion to model instructional practices and as resources/mentors for general education teachers.

Benefits

- Encourages use of a variety of strategies to engage students in learning, which leads to increased achievement and decreased disciplinary problems
- Provides versatile learning modalities
- Provides support for students with special needs in inclusive general education classrooms
- Increases student engagement, which leads to increased achievement
- Increases teacher satisfaction, which leads to greater retention
- Emphasizes the shift from teaching to learning
- Encourages increased ownership of learning by students as they see meaning in the learning

Challenges

- Budgeting for professional development and finding appropriate professional development providers
- Creating a variety of assessments, providing planning time, developing appropriate materials, and so on
- Helping teachers break from old patterns and broaden their ideas about how to teach and provide for individual differences

Progress Measures

- Collect and analyze student engagement data (observation) to document the degree of student involvement and engagement and compare individual increases in engagement with documented individual student achievement increases (student assessment analysis) and disciplinary referral decreases (discipline analysis).
- Document increased use of learning style inventories, multiple intelligence strategies, and responsive teaching strategies.
- Verify teachers' use of alternative assessments, such as student portfolio reviews and exhibitions.

RECOMMENDATION 25: Teachers design and use formative and summative assessments to inform instruction, advance learning, accommodate individual learning needs, and monitor student progress.

Strategies

- Use formative assessments to guide instructional planning, focus review efforts, and target interventions.
- View assessment as an opportunity to teach.
- Shift perceptions and practices of assessment from judging to supporting and advancing learning.
- Use student portfolios and assess them regularly with each student.
- Create small-scale diagnostic assessments to evaluate student learning and weaknesses and modify instruction accordingly.
- Create common assessments across grade levels and content areas.
- Provide staff development in the use of assessment as a diagnostic tool.
- Include interactive lessons and simulations that assess students on the basis of their individual skills and abilities.
- Align classroom assessment rubrics with state assessment rubrics.
- Encourage students to generate questions according to their familiarity with rubrics and state standards.
- Use "backward planning" in designing units. (See the work of Wiggins and McTighe.)

Benefits

- Encourages the use of diagnostic assessments that allow teachers to adjust instruction to meet student needs in identified areas
- Changes the dynamic of assessment so that students begin to see it as a regular part of the learning experience
- Provides an opportunity for students to become familiar with the format and, to a certain extent, the content of state and national assessments
- Allows teachers to design and use assessment and instructional strategies that focus on individual learning abilities and intelligences

Challenges

- Providing time and resources for professional development on alternative assessments
- Overcoming resistance to new practices
- Developing diagnostic assessments
- Developing common assessments
- Helping students see assessment as helpful to their growth, rather than something to be feared
- Addressing the time-consuming nature of student participation in multiple assessments as the lesson progresses
- Dispelling the myth that assessment is an intrusion on instructional time

Progress Measures

- Include self-evaluation and self-reflection by students as part of their portfolio reviews.
- Document teachers' articulation of goals, objectives, and benchmarks for courses and units, as well as teaching strategies and assessments.

CURRICULUM, INSTRUCTION, AND ASSESSMENT

WHAT?

CURRICULUM, INSTRUCTION, AND ASSESSMENT

WHAT?

RECOMMENDATION 26: Each educator possesses pedagogical expertise, a broad academic foundation, in-depth content knowledge in the subjects taught, and an understanding of the developmental needs of his or her students.

Strategies

- Hire only qualified and certified teachers.
- Ensure that teachers are assigned to teach subjects for which they are qualified and certified.
- Encourage teachers to expand their knowledge in an area of interest in their discipline, pursue advanced degrees, or gain certification in additional subject areas.
- Provide ongoing, job-embedded professional development for all teachers that:
  - Maintains and improves instructional and assessment skills
  - Ensures a clear understanding of the developmental needs of the students they are teaching
  - Promotes an understanding of student diversity
  - Provides skills in promoting positive student behavior.
- Encourage active participation in professional discipline–specific associations as well as in other professional organizations.
- Provide additional support for teachers, regardless of experience, who are changing schools, grade levels, or subject areas.

Benefits

- Ensures higher quality instruction for students
- Supports the imperative that at least one person on each academic team has in-depth knowledge in each academic field
- Supports student learning to a higher degree when teachers have broad academic knowledge
- Encourages teachers to work with colleagues to integrate the curriculum

Challenges

- Confronting the serious teacher shortage—especially where emergency certification is the norm—and the competition from other schools (public, private, and charter) for the best teacher candidates
- Addressing the reality that highly qualified teachers demand higher salaries
- Scheduling that too often assigns teachers to classes in subject areas where they are not certified or qualified
- Differing certification standards from state to state

Progress Measures

- Document a decrease in the percentage of teachers teaching "out of field" each year.
- Require a personal learning plan from each teacher each year, including documentation of newly researched areas in his or her field as evidence of ongoing personal professional development.
- Administer an end-of-year survey to teachers that includes specific items related to teacher satisfaction. Correlate results to satisfaction (morale) issues. Compare with actual teacher turnover and substantiate by conducting exit interviews using the same questions.

RECOMMENDATION 27: Teachers promote active engagement of each student in his or her own learning through coaching and facilitating.

Strategies

- Provide teachers with professional development in how to facilitate, coach, and guide rather than lecture.
- Use integrated course work, project-based learning, and service learning to engage students.
- Require student portfolios, student-led conferences, and exhibitions that are open to the community when appropriate.
- Adopt programs that are designed to promote active learning.
- Provide students with choices in studies, projects, and assessments.
- Incorporate student choice and interests into the curriculum.

Benefits

- Increases student engagement, satisfaction, and achievement
- Allows for differentiated instruction
- Decreases discipline problems
- Improves teacher satisfaction when all students can demonstrate individual and group comprehension of a topic or lesson
- Promotes independence for students with special needs while fostering collaboration

Challenges

- Providing funding, resources, and released time for training
- Moving teachers away from lecture-driven teaching styles
- Redesigning instruction to promote active learning
- Understanding how to determine and address each student's readiness, interest, and learning profile
- Addressing the everyday challenges, such as behavioral problems, absences, and the like

Progress Measures

- Conduct regular classroom observations to measure the amount of class time spent in active learning as opposed to lecture or nonactive learning activities.
- Survey students and teachers to assess the success and impact of programs.
- Review sample teacher-administered assessments to ensure that they are geared toward specific modalities.

CURRICULUM, INSTRUCTION, AND ASSESSMENT

WHAT?

RECOMMENDATION 28: The school ensures a smooth academic and social transition for each student from grade to grade and school to school.

Strategies

- Communicate regularly with all schools within the district or attendance pattern.
- Promote visits and other interactions with institutions of higher education.
- Develop an articulated K–12 curriculum that identifies the essential learnings for each grade level.
- Encourage regular cross-grade and cross-school communications among teachers and principals.
- Provide opportunities for students and parents to visit and interact with adults and students from the receiving school.
- Use the first day of the new school year as an orientation time for students new to the school with returning students starting a day later.
- Communicate regularly with parents of students from the sending schools well before transitions occur.

Benefits

- Lessens students' fear and confusion about what is expected at each level
- Improves parents' understanding of expectations
- Provides specific information about student mastery so that teachers can plan instruction to ensure that students are where they need to be at the end of the year
- Decreases time needed to diagnose the learning needs of incoming students, leading to more efficient use of the school year
- Allows students to spend more time learning and less time transitioning

Challenges

- Providing staff time and funding
- Finding common planning time for teachers in different buildings and at different grade levels
- Coming to consensus about appropriate expectations for the level of mastery
- Setting up a vertical system and operating it smoothly, which takes a number of years to achieve

Progress Measures

- Provide evidence of systematic planning and communication between and among all school units at both the program and individual student level.
- Review and revise orientation program, administrative and teacher articulation meetings, and transition plans.
- Solicit narrative descriptions from students and family members on the transition issues encountered when moving from one school level to another.
- Enlist content specialists to review and make suggestions regarding articulation plans.

RECOMMENDATION 29: The staff and students use current technology to improve instruction, enhance individualized learning, and facilitate management and operations.

Strategies

- Develop a budget that allows the school to update technology on an ongoing basis.
- Develop partnerships with businesses to provide technology support.
- Provide ongoing professional development for teachers to integrate technology into the curriculum, instruction, and assessment.
- Encourage teachers to individualize instruction and assessment through the use of technology.
- Write grant proposals to fund technology initiatives.
- Create a technology team that develops a plan to guide the goals, purchase, and use of technology for classroom and schoolwide use.
- Develop polices that promote student use of technology, the Internet, and social media in a responsible and productive manner.

Benefits

- Enables the use of a more diverse set of educational programs and products
- Promotes the active engagement of students in their learning
- Teaches students skills that will be required throughout their lifetimes
- Helps to individualize learning for each student, with accommodations for those with special needs
- Provides relevance to learning

Challenges

- Ensuring that the school has the capacity to keep up with the constant evolution of technology
- Finding the time, money, training, and resources for ongoing support
- Accepting student use of personal technology as an educational advantage
- Motivating teachers to become tech-savvy and view technology skills as critical to student success

Progress Measures

- Document schoolwide adoption of a technology plan with clear standards of use, assessments of effectiveness, plans for periodic updates of hardware and software, and a sound program to protect students from inappropriate material.
- Collect evidence of teacher participation in an ongoing professional development program in the area of technology (record of activities, teacher participation, and mastery of objectives).
- Document technology integration, as appropriate, in teachers' daily lessons (observation).
- Measure the increased use of technology by students in their academic work.
- Compile evidence that the development of partnerships and location of grants to support technology initiatives has been undertaken by the technology team.

CURRICULUM, INSTRUCTION, AND ASSESSMENT

WHAT?

Promoting Discussion Around "What"
What Needs to Improve?

What we do to improve student learning is as important as how we go about creating change. Process is important in any endeavor of merit; however, in school improvement, just as in cooking, the ingredients in the recipe are equally important.

- Once your team has collected data, analyzed it, and established priorities for action, what strategies and course of action will you take to address specific needs?
- How will you engage a cross section of the school community in the conversation about the possibilities?
- How will your team ensure that each strategy you consider includes elements of the three core areas of the *Breaking Ranks* Framework?
- What role will the cornerstones for success play in your examination of different programs, strategies, and processes? How will your team address elements of those cornerstones in exploring possible solutions and deciding on a course of action?
- How will the capacity of the school community members to effectively perform the roles required for implementing the initiative and their need for professional development impact your team's final decision about specific approaches?
- How will your team involve students and parents in the exploration and decision making about possible solutions?
- How will your team assess the capacity of existing structures and processes in your school to support the effective implementation of the strategy you select to address the school's prioritized needs? How will you go about creating new structures and operational process to support teachers, students, parents, and leaders as the initiative progresses?

How?

CHAPTER 3

HOW DO WE IMPROVE OUR SCHOOL?
THE PROCESS DEFINED

Despite a long history of reforms, not every school has arrived at the point of serving each student. Every school leader has studied and reviewed plans or implemented reforms that were thoughtful initiatives and promised substantive impact, but the results were less remarkable than expected, or worse, there were unintended and unanticipated consequences as a result of how they were implemented.

How a plan is implemented has a direct effect on school culture. A plan that is implemented poorly has as much long-term impact on that culture as one that is implemented properly. By the same token, the school culture influences the plan and the process. Suffice it to say that if your culture is not accepting of innovation, then your leadership team has some work to do.

This section is designed to help school leaders not only implement changes in structure, policies, and practices but also move beyond those and delve deeply into the mission, values, beliefs, and goals that compose the culture of the school. Without an emphasis on changing school culture, the ability of any single reform to be sustained and to improve learning for each student will be severely compromised and most likely doomed. The school's leadership team should use this section to promote collaboration and professional conversations among staff members—and between high school, middle level, and elementary staffs—that move beyond the basics of curriculum articulation and emphasize the additional importance of personalizing the learning and the school experience for each student at all grade levels.

As you guide your school from a business-as-usual mentality to one of continuous improvement, your team would be well advised to focus on shared vision and collaborative leadership. Schools are complex social systems and every school is unique. Two schools with similar demographic profiles often function much differently from each other. Literacy, science, and math programs that worked well in one school may achieve only marginal success in others. Approaches must be adapted to the complexities of the individual school or the good ideas will never be put into practice. Changing the culture of a school—trying to effect synchronous schoolwide change—is at best a risky proposition. Teachers have seen leaders and fads come and go, so they are appropriately skeptical. Leaders can't afford big mistakes, yet improved teaching and learning requires leaders to take risks and encourage innovation.

Culture is like the auto-pilot or mind-set of a school. It is a combination of all the attitudes, beliefs, and values that guide the behavior of those in the school. Unless that underlying mind-set is changed, the school will return to its prior ways of operating and no real change will take place. For example, some researchers believe that punitive grading systems are a major contributor to decreased student motivation. In response to an effort to change the grading system, teachers who believe that grades are a lever to force students into improving will behave one way. Teachers who believe that grades are tools to use to encourage students to learn and improve will behave in a quite different manner. Unless the whole staff develops the same mind-set about grading and the purpose of grading, little real change will take place.

The good news is that educators don't have to learn by trial-and-error. They can learn from other people's experiences, but only if they understand what will work for their school and implement it at the right time and with careful preparation of staff members. Remember, no plan, program, or initiative will work unless the staff will "work the plan."

Relationships Open the Door

Relationships are important in everyone's personal and professional life. Think for a moment about your personal interactions with friends or family. Even the most commonplace events—a dinner, a trip to the store with the kids, an afternoon hike—have the opportunity to foster dynamic relationships and lasting memories that can maintain those relationships during challenging times. How you conduct yourselves during those commonplace events is often significantly more important than what you are actually doing. Likewise, in professional interactions, the "how" is just as important—even when undertaking activities that are routine.

It is how we address the commonplace—the seemingly minor initiatives or small changes—that will allow more significant activities to occur. Those minor initiatives no longer seem minor when they foster a culture capable of tackling larger initiatives. Once the leadership team has helped create that culture—one that believes that each student can achieve at high levels—external influences or a change of principal may have less impact.

Success Relies on "How"

Whether you work in a school that is considered "in need of improvement" or a school where things are going relatively well or even very well, closing the achievement gap and addressing the needs of each student should be the centerpiece of your planning. Where does a leadership team start? Let's say, for example, that your leadership team and staff members have examined the data and planned a course of action that is based on sound educational principles and what the team and staff members think is best for students. But things feel disconnected—as if you are stringing together a series of actions and programs but getting nowhere. Although many of the things you are trying may be good in and of themselves, without a master plan connected to a vision, it's like trying to put together a giant jigsaw puzzle without the picture on the box to guide you.

Many educators, when presented with good data, may agree on what needs to be done to turn things around (e.g., effective teaming, flexible scheduling, advisories, and differentiated

Figure 3.1

20% of Successful Implementation Relies on What	80% of Successful Implementation Relies on How
Differentiated instruction	Data collection and accurate analysis
Personal learning plans	Collaborative and distributed leadership
Advisories	Readiness assessment and ability to build capacity
Common planning time	Values alignment
Flexible scheduling	Professional development
Activities/services tied to learning	Project management
K–16 continuity	Communication and "buy-in"
Small units	Role clarity and design
Real-world application	Monitoring and adjustment

instruction). Why is it then that most major change initiatives do not meet expectations or fail outright, whether in education, business, nonprofits, or government organizations? In most cases, it's not that people weren't smart enough, didn't agree on what should be done, or didn't have the best of intentions. The reason is more commonly that they didn't know how to implement change effectively and how to sustain it.

Success is dependent mostly on how things are done and, in particular, how effective communication is, how much buy-in is obtained, and the degree to which everyone understands how roles will change as the initiatives are implemented. An authoritative leader can get something in place by decree, but it won't be implemented correctly and likely won't be sustained. The items in the left column in Figure 3.1 are reflective of the what—the initiative that was selected to improve student outcomes. Although you can't move forward until the what is set, the items in the right column—the how—are the primary determinants of your success, the key change process elements.

When people reflect on initiatives that didn't meet expectations or were dropped after a short while, they will invariably identify one or more of the items in the right column as being the primary cause. The tragedy is that with every failed initiative, the "change-history bank account" decreases in value, making the chance of success for the next change initiative even slimmer. Implementing initiatives according to a well-defined process is crucial. Mihalic, Irwin, Fagan, Ballard, and Elliott (2004) wrote:

> Discovering what works does not solve the problem of program effectiveness. Once models and best practices are identified, practitioners are faced with the challenge of implementing programs properly. A poorly implemented program can lead to failure as easily as a poorly designed one. (p. 95)

Rumberger (2009) and many other researchers and program developers agree that it is important for school personnel to implement a program with a high degree of fidelity. In general, the better the fidelity, the better the student outcomes. Despite this, research has demonstrated that a large percentage of teachers who implement programs add or delete items upon implementation (i.e., adaptation), change components or procedures over time (i.e., drift), or discontinue their use. When implementing a new program, it is important to understand that although adaptation may be effective in some cases, if staff alter or stray too much from the implementation procedures used in the validation research, their changes could affect the approach's effectiveness and may consequently cause the approach to fail.

> Our failure to improve schools in the last few decades isn't because we lack funding or don't know how to improve schools. What we lack is the "will and persistence" to implement what we already know.
>
> (Odden, 2009, p. 22)

Solo versus Team: Starting Off on the Right Foot

So where does your school start? The *Breaking Ranks* Process Circle will help teams decide where to start and what steps should be incorporated into any reform initiative. There are many seemingly justifiable reasons that one might try to go solo rather than collaborate: a belief in a moral imperative to make change any way possible, a principal new to the school with a mandate to shake things up, a failure to meet adequate yearly progress (AYP), the perceived inertia of staff members, and so on. Unfortunately, reform history demonstrates that improvements derived from changes forced from the top will likely be short-lived. The process circle is designed to help you avoid this pitfall and work with others to create a climate and culture that will foster significant and sustainable change.

The goal of the principal and leadership team should not be to get everyone to toe their line, but to arrive at a line together. The more leaders that are included—among staff members and students—the more sustainable the thrust for excellence in your school will be. That type of collaborative leadership will also create the climate and conditions for optimum performance. Changing the attitudes, values, and beliefs that drive a school requires courage and effort. Underpinning this shift must be the core belief that each student should be challenged to achieve at high levels.

If changes in school culture are to occur, all efforts must be collaborative in nature, but that does not diminish the role of the principal as the leader of the process. Furthermore, although communication and buy-in are essential, there are times when consensus cannot be reached by a larger team, which may require that the leadership team make a decision. Because culture is driven by the physical conditions, rules, policies, practices, and the like that affect it, an open discussion of what will change and how it will change is necessary. Making decisions transparent is essential to the success of any endeavor.

Teams and their performance are crucial to your school's success. In the past, schools were judged on the performance of individuals. Their task was to sort students for success and their reputations rested upon a few star teachers who were masters of their crafts but operated as independent contractors. Today, schools are judged by the achievement of all students. Success depends on the collective performance of the entire staff and teams of teachers working together to ensure the success of each student. The best school leaders create environments in which teams are able to flourish.

Leaders who believe in their staff members—that they are self-motivated, that better decisions are made collectively, and that buy-in and cooperation are more important than control—will promote a culture characterized by collaboration, trust, mutual respect, shared decision making, ownership, and shared responsibility. On the other hand, leaders who believe that people must be motivated, supervised, directed, and controlled will foster a hierarchical school culture characterized by top-down decision making, low levels of trust, and a focus on control (McGregor, 1985). Although the latter type of leadership may supply short-term results, it may also lead to long-term resistance in other areas and a lack of interest in sustaining important long-term reforms. Be it driven by new leadership, external mandates, or a new direction inspired by existing leadership, school improvement will only be effective if the proper conditions are created.

A Process to Build Culture and Achieve Results

Which comes first: creating a culture that will support a process of change or implementing a process that creates a culture to support change? The question is not the rhetorical chicken-and-egg debate. A highly influential and charismatic leader with a good plan might be able to begin to foster a culture of change; however, a process that fosters a culture of change while pursuing the goal of improved student performance will consistently produce more favorable conditions to realize goals.

A good process will have the ability to motivate the entire school team around initiatives that are aligned not for the improvement of culture alone, but ultimately for improved student performance. It is at that point of improved student performance that the interconnectedness of the three core areas of *Breaking Ranks*—collaborative leadership; personalizing your school environment; and curriculum, instruction and assessment—bring meaning to the process for change outlined in the process circle. By thoughtfully addressing each of the areas of the circles, you will be able to ensure that your initiatives have a well-defined process that not only allows you to implement initiatives but also to do so in a way that improves school culture and becomes sustainable.

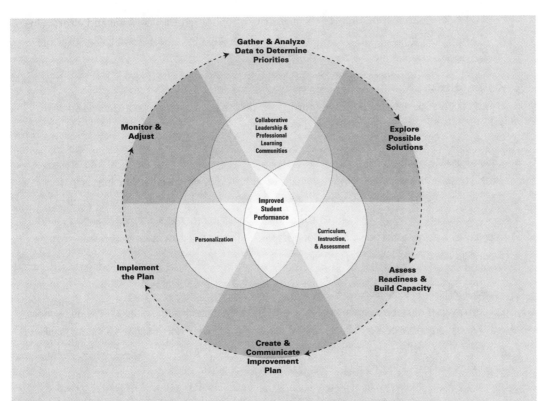

The Process to Break Ranks in Your School: A Synopsis

At the core, all efforts to change your school must ultimately be focused on improved student performance. To be successful, all steps of the *Breaking Ranks* change process must be based on a **shared vision**, promoted by **collaborative leadership**, and supported by **professional development**.

1. **Gather and Analyze Data to Determine Priorities**

    Carefully examine all available data to **determine priorities**. To paint an accurate big-picture look at the school, data must be gathered from a wide variety of sources and used to determine the areas of greatest need. To be effective the data must be personalized—faces must be put on the numbers.

    Gather Data:

    a. *Demographic data:* Ethnic population, mobility rate, poverty indicators, parents' education, housing, etc.

    b. *Academic data:* State test scores; other testing data (SAT, ACT, PSAT, etc.); district, school, and classroom assessments; failure rates; interim progress reports; observations of classroom practice—what's actually happening in the classroom; etc.

    c. *Diagnostic assessment data:* Reading, writing, mathematics (RTI)

    d. *Behavioral data:* Attendance, suspensions, referrals, expulsions, interventions, counselor visits, bullying issues, harassment, etc.

e. *Miscellaneous data:* NASSP satisfaction surveys (staff members, parents, students—visit www.nassp.org), surveys of businesses and community members, exit interviews and surveys, etc.

f. *Student perception data:* Student shadowing, student forums, for example, the model Raising Student Voice and Participation (RSVP) from NASSP and the National Association of Student Councils.

Analyze Data:

Sort by subgroups; look for patterns, growth, and declines over time and correlations across subjects; equity of access to challenging classes; etc.

2. **Explore Possible Solutions**

On the basis of the priorities derived from analyzing the data, **explore possible solutions** that will lead to improved student performance. Consider such categories as curriculum, instruction, assessment, professional development, equitable access to programs, academic support, and interventions as potential goal areas. Conduct site visits and talk with other school leaders. (See *Breaking Ranks II* and *Breaking Ranks in the Middle.*)

3. **Assess Readiness and Build Capacity**

Determine what must be in place in order to successfully implement the needed changes. **Assess** staff needs, organizational structures, programs, and curricula to determine the school's **readiness** and overall **capacity** to address the identified priorities. **Build capacity** to address these needs through training, reallocating resources, and revising schedules.

4. **Create and Communicate Improvement Plan**

On the basis of stakeholder input and the information gained from the previous step, establish goals for an **improvement plan** that is designed to improve student performance. Incorporate those goals into all aspects of school improvement planning and ensure clear **communication** with all involved parties.

5. **Implement the Plan**

Just do it! (See *Breaking Ranks II* and *Breaking Ranks in the Middle* for proven strategies to guide implementation.)

6. **Monitor and Adjust**

As the plan is implemented, determine regular checkpoints to **monitor** progress. Repeat surveys as appropriate. As additional data is collected and analyzed, make **adjustments** or refinements as needed. Be sure to share results and progress.

On the following pages each of the six stages of the process circle will be discussed in greater detail following the same format:

1. Discussion of that stage of the process circle.
2. Change leadership activities related to that stage of the process circle that your team can engage in to support culture shift and implementation.
3. A completed matrix of activities related to that stage of the process circle that your team should consider. The chart delineates a number of possible items to consider and explore within the following areas common to all stages:

   ■ Sources of data and analysis
   ■ Collaborative leadership
   ■ Infrastructure capacity
   ■ Communication and buy-in
   ■ Professional development

The sample matrix that follows offers ideas for you to consider; your team must complete individual matrix sheets that are based on local circumstances and the initiative considered. A blank matrix worksheet can be found in Appendix 4.

STAGE: Gather and Analyze Data to Determine Priorities

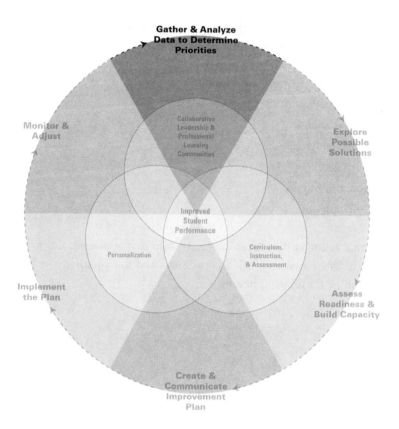

Good leaders are often good because they trust their intuition and use it to act quickly. It is difficult to put intuition on hold to take the time to identify and analyze data; however, when contemplating changes in your school that affect culture and how you do business on a day-to-day basis, data-based decision making is the hallmark of success.

Principals and teams who use intuition as a basis for starting a change effort are doomed to failure because the staff's first reaction will be, That's his (or her) opinion. Since opinions are like noses—everybody has one—you don't want to unintentionally misdirect the focus away from a worthy initiative because the staff is caught up in personalities.

Change Leadership Activities
Many initiatives fail because teams don't take the time and effort necessary to get buy-in and clarify team member and stakeholder roles. The typical pattern is to identify a goal and then act immediately—which leads to failure in most cases. There are two general types of data (i.e., cultural and project or challenge specific) that can be used by teams (either a leadership team or an initiative-specific *Breaking Ranks* [BR] team). For example, a principal or a leadership team might choose to use interviews or other informal information or data to get the pulse of the culture and climate before they ever gathered data related to addressing specific areas of concern. They would then use that data—or work with a *BR* team—to determine priorities and explore possible solutions.

1. **Data about the culture of the school.** Data on school culture can provide valuable information about what is feasible. Use that information to sketch out an initial goal and a process for validating and meeting the goal. The main objective is to create the right focus for change and to start building support for that change. The valuable by-product of this data collection, when done with sensitivity and tact, is the building of trust and credibility. Some of the keys to success at this stage of the change process include:

   - Treading softly—not beginning with preconceived ideas or pushing an agenda
   - Listening—gathering both formal and informal data from multiple sources
   - Identifying and speaking with staff members who will be candid and provide good data
   - Establishing preliminary performance baselines
   - Identifying causes for observed problems—for example, identifying the reasons students are not performing up to par
   - Building a preliminary case for change, including a cost-benefit analysis
   - Identifying a preliminary change goal to address issues
   - Identifying obstacles and potential sources of resistance
   - Creating a preliminary change process roadmap
   - Identifying potential resources and informal and formal change champions
   - Evaluating the adequacy of current communication vehicles to support a major change effort.

Making the Case for Gauging School Climate

To help schools draw staff members, students, and parents into a collaborative school improvement process, NASSP has created the Comprehensive Assessment of School Environment (CASE)—a series of perception surveys that are based on the concepts in the *Breaking Ranks* Framework. All survey items are focused around the three core areas of *Breaking Ranks*:

- Collaborative leadership
- Personalization
- Curriculum, instruction, and assessment.

CASE is designed to:

- Collect data about student, teacher, and parent satisfaction with a school's environment and culture
- Identify school strengths and areas for improvement
- Assist in designing a school improvement plan using the *Breaking Ranks* process circle
- Support planning, including budget decisions.

Made up of a student survey, a parent survey, and an instructional staff surveys, CASE gives stakeholders a valuable voice in school improvement and provides your school leadership team with data on:

- Stakeholder satisfaction with the status quo
- Perceived strengths and weaknesses of the school
- Areas for future improvement.

Visit www.nassp.org/case for more information.

Once your team gathers data related to culture, the *BR* team can proceed to gathering the data applicable to specific areas of change. This element of the change leadership process is crucial. If team development, communication and buy-in, and data collection processes are not done correctly from the start, the project's chance of success is significantly compromised. The team must communicate the need for change in the most compelling way possible.

2. **Data about performance or a specific area of strength or challenge.** The *BR* team will likely take the lead on this and may work closely with the leadership team. The questions in the following matrix delineate other items to consider as your team plans its activities around data.

General Questions for Your Team to Consider That May Require Data

These questions will help you review the data more carefully and systematically

- Is the culture truly student centered?
- Are good student and classroom practice data available?
- Are the data disaggregated?
- Are the data of sufficient quality and quantity to make good decisions?
- Are teams structured appropriately and are they performing well?
- What data is available regarding the extent to which staff members freely share information and practices?
- Is the staff performing at a high level as reflected by student outcomes?
- Is the workload reasonable and distributed equitably?
- Is the climate positive? (What data support this?)
- What is the school's change history?
- Who are the champions of change?
- Who can be trusted to provide good information?
- What are the sources of resistance to change?
- What resources are available to conduct a successful change process?
- What are the primary needs and issues?
- Does it make more sense to start small or to start big?
- What relevant data are available concerning the issues and goals we are addressing?
- If the data aren't available—for example, the quality and quantity is not sufficient for good decision making—what must be done to obtain them?
- Given the level of effort required, do we need a research/data subteam of the project team to do the work?
- What methodologies can we employ to understand the voice of the student—for example, student shadowing, student interviews and focus groups, student visioning exercises?
- Have we reviewed the *BR* recommendations to ensure that we are addressing the three core areas?

See *Breaking Ranks: A Field Guide for Leading Change* to review more excellent sources of data and how to retrieve it. Visit www.nassp.org/brguide.

Activities: Gather and Analyze Data to Determine Priorities

Sources of Data and Analysis	■ See *Breaking Ranks II*, pp. 26–31, and *Breaking Ranks in the Middle*, pp. 63–65.
	■ Establish and implement a formal data collection and analysis process. Often a subteam will conduct research and work with the school or district data team to obtain the required information.
	■ Identify disaggregated student outcome data to establish performance baselines. You may discover during this process that essential learnings have not been adequately established, which may become one of your major change goals. (See *Breaking Ranks II*, pp. 6–8, and *Breaking Ranks in the Middle*, pp. 8–10.)
	■ Evaluate classroom practices.
	■ Employ activities to collect the voice of the student and the voice of the parent.
Collaborative Leadership	■ Is decision making distributed appropriately across key stakeholders?
	■ Are meaningful tasks delegated for both implementation and development purposes?
	■ How can the selection of the initial team members reinforce collaborative leadership?
	■ What is the composition of the team? Are all key stakeholder groups represented? Are students on the team?
	■ Are students being given a leadership role in gathering data?
	■ Are students taking a leading role in obtaining data from their peers?
	■ Are students taking a leading role in presenting data to the team or other stakeholder groups?
	■ What is the principal's role in this change effort?
	■ Should the principal be part of the team? If so, in what role?
	■ Does the team have the authority to set final goals and to implement them?
	■ What approvals are needed from supervisors to move forward on the goals selected?
	■ What leadership support is required from the district to ensure success?
Infrastructure Capacity	■ Do systems, policies, and procedures help or hinder getting work done?
	■ Are resources allocated fairly and reasonably?
	■ What system improvements will be necessary to support a major change initiative?
	■ Do we need to set up any new systems to track relevant data? If so, do we have sufficient resources to do so?
	■ Are sufficient resources available to support the team and overall change effort? If not, what must be done to obtain them?

HOW?

Activities: Gather and Analyze Data to Determine Priorities

Communication and Buy-In	■ Have you:
	  ● Identified and prioritized stakeholders and their needs when it comes to communication and potential resistance to proposed goals?
	  ● Created and implemented an effective communication and buy-in plan that is based on your stakeholder analysis?
	  ● Created new communication vehicles (or used existing vehicles) to support the communication and buy-in plan?
	  ● Incorporated the case for change into the communication and buy-in plan?
	■ Are communications adequate?
	■ To what degree is the leadership team or *Breaking Ranks* team communicating appropriate expectations and providing encouragement for meeting our vision and mission?
	■ To what degree do members of the team model the values that are essential for success as an organization?
	■ How is the team viewed?
	■ Is the current level of trust and credibility sufficient to drive a major change initiative?
	■ If not, what needs to be done to strengthen how the change is viewed by others?
	■ To what degree have people bought into the need for change?
	■ Who are the stakeholders who will be most affected by the goals?
	■ Which stakeholders are likely to oppose the proposed changes?
	■ Who will own the communication and buy-in process for this project? An individual on the team? A subteam of the project team?
	■ What must be done to ensure that key stakeholders are brought on board?
	■ Have potential resistors been assigned to the project team or involved in the project in some way?

Professional Development	■ Is the staff receiving sufficient professional development to meet current goals? ■ What professional development might be necessary if a major change initiative were undertaken? ■ Who should be on the project team for development purposes? ■ What type of training does the team need to be effective in managing the change process, with regard to data collection and analysis, communication and buy-in strategies, and the goal selected? (For example, if a personalization goal—such as establishing an advisory program—were selected, what training and technical assistance would be required?)

Student Voice: A Critical, yet Often Overlooked Data Point

Just as students are often left out of discussions about their academic performance, so too are they sometimes neglected when it comes to issues of school climate, the curriculum, and a host of other issues that directly affect them. In so many instances, the bus schedule or the needs of adults dictate what happens to students—those silent partners in the educational process who legally have very little choice but to attend to whatever adults say.

Leadership teams must develop methods to find out what students are thinking and what their interests are. In addition to personal learning plans, advisories and student membership on leadership teams or school boards, consider Raising Student Voice and Participation (RSVP), an initiative of NASSP and the National Association of Student Councils (NASC).

RSVP is a student engagement program aligned with the *Breaking Ranks* Framework that can be easily integrated into existing student council programs. Student leaders facilitate a series of small group student summits that engage the entire student body in dialogue to see what ideas the students have for community and school improvement. RSVP can provide the leadership team with an invaluable source of data that students will develop and compile, and it allows the leadership team to address specific concerns revealed by the data.

As important, the students are asked by their peers to develop proposals—and to volunteer their time and talent to being part of any solution that the principal or the school leadership team determines is actionable. Consequently, students are given opportunities to produce results within the community and within the school—but only if they put in the necessary effort.

RSVP helps schools encourage students to be partners in the school change process and will enable leadership teams to understand the school, community, and global issues that concern students the most. RSVP also:

- Provides principals with a way to utilize the leadership of their student councils to engage students more and personalize their school experience
- Involves every student and all student populations, specifically giving those students who are typically not involved an opportunity to share their voices and participate in civic-based activities
- Establishes a process and framework for developing and implementing student-directed projects
- Brings abstract learning to life.

The "simple" act of giving every student a voice—the goal of RSVP—is in and of itself a step toward changing the culture of the school. (Visit www.nasc.us/rsvp.)

RSVP supports *Breaking Ranks* Framework recommendations with a focus on:
- Meaningful decision-making roles for students
- A set of core values that are essential in a democratic and civil society
- Diversity and an array of viewpoints (especially from students who are not typically heard)
- Extended academic learning and personal development through service learning, community service, and student activities
- Active engagement in learning
- Shared vision
- Collaborative development of learning goals and an improvement plan
- Partnerships with community
- A safe, caring environment
- Smooth academic and social transitions
- Curriculum connections to real-life applications and extended learning beyond the campus.

STAGE: Explore Possible Solutions

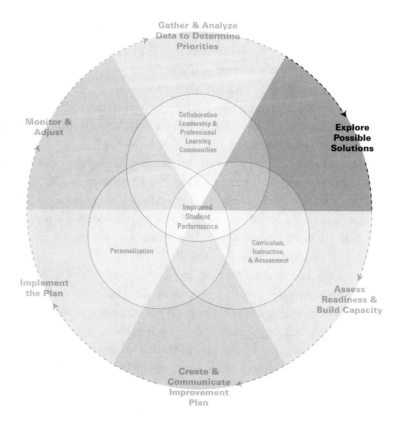

You've scanned your environment, pulled a *BR* team together, delved into the data, identified the issues, and established some preliminary goals. If you are action oriented, a trait of most successful school leaders, the temptation to grab a solution and head to the races is almost too powerful to overcome. But overcome it you must! Will your team be able to control the impulse to rush, or will it take the time to do a thorough investigation of which approach will best address your issues and meet your goals and ultimately turn that approach into a compelling change vision for your school?

Change Leadership Activities

This element of the change leadership process focuses on the generation of multiple approaches for addressing the issues and goals you identified on the basis of your data analysis. It ensures that no stone is unturned in selecting the best approach for your issues, goals, and school culture. It is important at this time to keep an open mind about what might work in your environment. People don't know what they don't know, but they can become informed of their options so that the best ones can be selected. Each of the multiple approaches considered must be grounded in sound educational research.

When your team has landed on the approach that best meets your needs, you must create a compelling vision of your goals and why the approach selected is the one that will bring results. Some of the keys to success include investigating a wide range of options:

- Involving people in activities they enjoy, such as school site visits, research on best practices, interviews, focus groups, speaking with experts, attending workshops and showcases, etc.
- Involving others—those not on the *BR* team—in the investigation process (e.g., inviting them to join a subteam) that will also support the buy-in process
- Developing sophisticated communication processes
- Creating and employing a clear set of criteria to evaluate each option's fit for your school
- Creating a compelling vision for the future of your school once the final approaches have been selected.

Activities: Explore Possible Solutions

The following matrix reflects those core change leadership elements and questions that surface during the data-gathering stage of the change process. Each section of the process circle has a similar matrix. *(The list below is a sample and is not intended to provide all of the information for any given initiative. Tailor it to your school's needs.)* The *BR* team should discuss and complete the activities matrix in each chapter. This exercise will help to ensure that your team has considered most areas related to the initiative. An example of a combined activity chart can be found in the schoolwide literacy initiative matrix on p. 100.

<table>
<tr>
<td rowspan="5">Essential Elements of Each Step</td>
<td>Sources of Data and Analysis</td>
<td>
<ul>
<li>Have you reviewed all the BR strategies and recommendations?</li>
<li>Have all the possible solution approaches/options been identified for data collection—e.g., curriculum; instruction; assessment; scheduling; professional development; equitable access to programs; academic support; and specific programs, such as advisories or student-led conferences?</li>
<li>Have data collection protocols been created when investigating different options. For example, is there a protocol for school site visits or for the analysis of presentations at school showcases?</li>
<li>Have clear criteria been created for evaluating options with regard to their potential for meeting your school's needs?</li>
<li>Have team members been trained in how to use the criteria to evaluate the options?</li>
</ul>
</td>
</tr>
<tr>
<td>Collaborative Leadership</td>
<td>
<ul>
<li>Are you able to offer different stakeholders leadership roles in the investigation of options? For example, have you assigned a leader to the school site visit team or assigned a leader of a research team who will be scouring the literature for options that have been successful in schools like yours?</li>
<li>Have people been assigned to take a lead in communicating findings to stakeholders?</li>
<li>What role are students playing at this stage in the process?</li>
<li>Have you considered putting students in charge of any of the site visit teams?</li>
<li>Have you considered having students do site visit report presentations?</li>
<li>Have you invited students from other schools to do presentations to your staff members on successful programs in their schools?</li>
</ul>
</td>
</tr>
<tr>
<td>Infrastructure Capacity</td>
<td>
<ul>
<li>As you look at options, are you considering how they will affect job roles, policies, procedures, and other practices?</li>
<li>Do any of the options being considered require a change in your communication or decision-making structures?</li>
</ul>
</td>
</tr>
<tr>
<td>Communication and Buy-In</td>
<td>
<ul>
<li>Are you keeping up with your communication requirements?</li>
<li>Are you sitting down with key stakeholders, particularly those who are resistant, to keep them on board with your efforts?</li>
<li>On the basis of the options selected, have you created a truly compelling vision of how those options will meet your goals?</li>
</ul>
</td>
</tr>
<tr>
<td>Professional Development</td>
<td>
<ul>
<li>Have people been given the skills necessary to collect data on different approaches/options.</li>
<li>Have they been trained on how to use data collection protocols?</li>
</ul>
</td>
</tr>
</table>

STAGE: Assess Readiness and Build Capacity

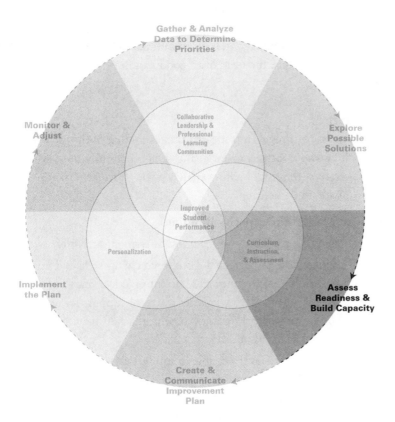

By this point, your *BR* team is well on its way to meeting its change expectations, after it has set goals that are based on good data and identified an approach and intervention options that will meet the school's needs. If the team has involved key stakeholders in the process and communicated effectively, it has created some buy-in for the goals and approach. But rest assured, not everyone will be on board yet with what your team plans to do. They may feel that the goals and approach make sense, but they may still have concerns about the team's ability to implement it well and to sustain it. In addition, there will be concerns (often unspoken) about what the change will mean for them personally with regard to their roles, relationships, skill requirements, and the amount of work they are going to be asked to do. They will also be looking for evidence that this new approach will work. Finally, even if the team has done everything right so far, this is the point where the initiative or team may have to pay for the decisions—and sometimes mistakes—of the past.

The question becomes, Why didn't some of these seemingly good initiatives work and become sustainable at this school? In many cases, it was not because the school was not ready but rather because the people were not prepared and the capacity had not been built to a point to effectively implement and sustain the change.

There are several types of readiness that must be evaluated and responded to in preparation for change. The first, as noted above, is related to buy-in. If your school has a negative change history and your staff is not ready to embrace the change, they will resist one way or another—actively or passively. The second has to do with role clarity. The team must ensure that everyone whose role is being affected by the change has a thorough understanding of what they are to do differently, what they are no longer supposed to do, and what knowledge and skills are required to be successful. The third has to do with infrastructure capacity. If goals and how work gets done are changing, then work processes, policies, procedures, and practices must be modified accordingly. And if those adjustments are significant, the organizational and communication structures may need to be adjusted as well. Once the team has a good handle on the level of readiness, it can build capacity where necessary.

Change Leadership Activities

This element of the change process requires a sophisticated understanding of the scope of the potential impacts of your goals and approach. A major change will touch just about every aspect of your school's operations; therefore, the risk of failure is high if you don't pay attention to the ripple effects of the change you are implementing.

Communication and Buy-In: Leadership Capacity Building

- Involve stakeholders—including students—in readiness assessment activities.
- Encourage teachers to evaluate how important the proposed changes are and how much of a perceived gap there is between importance and current practice. (Large gaps between perceived importance and current practice will garner the most support for action. Keep in mind that the leadership team's perceptions and those of the staff may differ; address that discrepancy so as not to create resistance.)
- Enhance collaborative leadership wherever possible to support the changes by redefining roles, conducting orientation sessions about the roles, and providing the professional development necessary to help staff members succeed in those roles.
- Provide frequent communications to the whole school community on the assessment and capacity-building process.

Role Clarity

Involve stakeholders in the role change analysis and redefinition process.

Educate everyone on which roles will change and which will not and provide a clear picture of new role requirements. For example, if your school is implementing a schoolwide literacy initiative, all teachers should understand that they are teachers of reading—responsible for teaching the language of their course and helping students understand vocabulary and course content.

Infrastructure Capacity Building

- Analyze how your goals will change the way work gets done across the organization.
- Establish current performance baselines in those areas affected by your goals.
- Conduct an "off the plate" analysis to adjust priorities and to free up time and resources to support goal attainment. (Seldom do organizations take the time to analyze what activities should be stopped to make time for new activities.)
- Adjust processes, policies, procedures, practices, and structures to support and sustain goal attainment.

Capacity building is most effective when all priorities are abundantly clear and resources can be allocated appropriately. In most cases, new initiatives cannot be added without consolidating efforts or eliminating other duties. To gain full commitment to a new initiative, it is important to identify what is no longer required—what people can take off the plate. This can only be done when priorities have been established. The team must clarify all of the demands that are planned and in play at any one time. This allows for appropriate prioritization and resource allocation. As you review these, it would be helpful to engage in an initiative mapping exercise that includes:

Brainstorming. Brainstorm all the initiatives—mandated and self-generated— that you are dealing with. Place each initiative on a separate sticky note and then place it on one of three flipcharts reflecting a time frame: current/short-term, medium-term, and long-term.

Prioritizing. Rank the initiatives in each time period according to its impact on student performance (e.g., academic, civic, social-emotional, postsecondary readiness, etc.).

Analyzing resistance. For each initiative, indicate the amount of resistance expected (low, medium, high) and the owner of each initiative (all noted on the flip charts).

Identifying implications. Given your analysis, identify the implications for the new initiatives you are planning and write them on a flipchart. Be sure to note where consolidation or elimination of initiatives is appropriate.

Presenting. Be prepared to present your results.

Activities: Assess Readiness and Build Capacity

The following matrix reflects those core change leadership elements and questions that surface during the Assess Readiness and Build Capacity stage of the change process. Each section of the process circle has a similar matrix. *(The list below is a sample and is not intended to provide all of the information for any given initiative. Tailor it to your school's needs.)* The *BR* team should discuss and complete the activities matrix in each chapter. This exercise will help to ensure that your team has considered most areas related to the initiative. An example of a combined activity chart can be found in the schoolwide literacy initiative matrix on p. 100.

<table>
<tr>
<td rowspan="5" style="writing-mode: vertical-rl">Essential Elements of Each Step</td>
<td>Sources of Data and Analysis</td>
<td>
■ What type of data do you need to assess readiness?
■ What tools and processes will you employ to assess readiness for change?
■ Have you identified all aspects of your school's functioning that will be affected by the change: process, policy, procedure, practice, structure, resource allocation, staffing, curriculum, etc.?
■ Have you identified what will no longer need to be done once the initiative has been implemented?
</td>
</tr>
<tr>
<td>Collaborative Leadership</td>
<td>
■ What opportunities exist for shared leadership at this stage of the change process?
■ Are the current leadership capacity development activities sufficient to support the effective implementation of the goals?
■ What leadership development will be required to *meet* the goals?
■ What leadership development will be required to *sustain* the goals?
■ What role can your students play in assessing readiness and building capacity?
■ Do you have students who are willing to play a part in the professional development of teachers?
</td>
</tr>
<tr>
<td>Infrastructure Capacity</td>
<td>
■ Are the resources adequate to support the change?
■ To what degree will reallocation of existing resources be needed?
■ What process, policy, procedure, practice, and structural changes are necessary to support the goals?
■ If major system/infrastructure changes are required, what sequence is needed to tackle them and how long will the capacity building process take?
■ Are the roles that will change because of the proposed changes be clear to everyone?
■ Do you have a methodology for conducting an effective role-redesign process?
</td>
</tr>
<tr>
<td>Communication and Buy-In</td>
<td>
■ Are as many stakeholders as reasonable involved in the readiness-assessment and capacity-building process?
■ Are the communication requirements being met?
■ Are key stakeholders, particularly those who are resistant, involved sufficiently to keep them on board with the efforts?
■ Is the team taking the temperature of the organization regarding the planned changes?
■ Are all the key stakeholders real partners in the change process at this point? If not, what must be done to get to that level of mutual support?
</td>
</tr>
<tr>
<td>Professional Development</td>
<td>
■ What specific capacity development is required for critical groups, such as teachers and administrators?
■ Is it clear what development is needed first, second, third, etc.?
■ Has the team created an overall staff development plan?
</td>
</tr>
</table>

HOW?

STAGE: Create and Communicate Improvement Plan

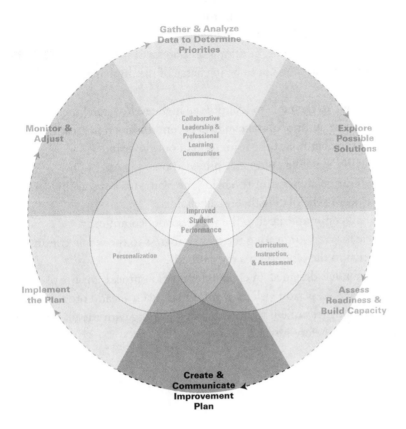

The *BR* team now has all the information it needs to craft and execute an implementation plan. The goals are clear and the readiness assessment has pointed out what capacity building is necessary to get the ball rolling. Once again, the temptation is to race to the finish line. Caution: resources will always be in short supply and buy-in will always be an issue. Managing resources and buy-in requires a good plan and excellent communication. If you are like most of us, you have been exposed to planning that has been less than effective or motivating, as reflected below in the words of an assistant principal:

> Planning is a royal pain…and a waste of time. When you're done, it doesn't do anything but confirm what you already knew. I don't think I've ever seen a plan get used. It's put in a drawer until it's time to dust it off and create a new one. People go off and do what they were going to do anyway. Now, you tell me, is that worth spending my time on?

Does this sentiment sound familiar? Even those people who plan well admit that planning is a chore—but an essential one when instituting changes that will have a significant impact. Planning is not a goal unto itself. Plan only to the degree necessary to meet the goals and ensure that what goes into the plan is relevant. Proper planning will help meet and sustain goals through the appropriate allocation of resources and buy-in by those affected by implementation. It may help avoid being blindsided and provide contingencies for managing the risks associated with change.

Change Leadership Activities

This element of the process provides a safety net. It ensures that the basics have been covered with regard to resources, buy-in, and unforeseen factors that might disrupt goal attainment. The plan can be created quickly, but carefully examining and reviewing the plan will take some time and requires good presentation and communication skills. Some of the keys to success are:

1. Designate someone on the *BR* team to be in charge of the implementation planning process.

2. Bring the right people to the table to identify the high level/overarching steps of the plan. This may include additional stakeholders beyond those on the team.

3. Get an individual or subgroup of the team to flesh out the plan.

4. Refine the plan with the whole group that provided the high-level steps.

5. Create a communication strategy for reviewing the plan with key stakeholders.

6. Examine every aspect of the plan with key stakeholders.

7. Refine the plan and communicate it to the whole school community.

8. Establish a vehicle for communicating the plan's progress to the whole community (school and external to the school) on a regular basis.

9. Ensure that the team has designed an effective evaluation process for the plan.

10. Designate a debugger—a person well known for finding errors and problems with existing systems. The debugger's role is to find out what's wrong with the plan so that corrections can be made to it before it is shared.

Activities: Create and Communicate Improvement Plan

The following matrix reflects those core change leadership elements and questions that surface during the Create and Communicate Improvement Plan stage of the change process. Each section of the process circle has a similar matrix. *(The list below is a sample and is not intended to provide all of the information for any given initiative. Tailor it to your school's needs.)* The *BR* team should discuss and complete the activities matrix in each chapter. This exercise will help ensure that your team has considered most areas related to the initiative. An example of a combined activity chart can be found in the schoolwide literacy initiative matrix on p. 100.

<table>
<tr>
<td rowspan="5">Essential Elements of Each Step</td>
<td>Sources of Data and Analysis</td>
<td>
■ What measures have been identified or created to track program impact?
■ What system has been designed to capture data once implementation has been started to evaluate if the program is meeting goals?
</td>
</tr>
<tr>
<td>Collaborative Leadership</td>
<td>
■ What opportunities exist to share leadership at this stage of the change process?
■ Have volunteers taken leadership roles concerning key aspects of implementation?
■ What leadership development will be required to meet the goals?
■ What leadership development will be required to sustain the goals?
■ What role can your students play in assessing readiness and building capacity?
■ Do you have students who are willing to play a part in the professional development of teachers?
</td>
</tr>
<tr>
<td>Infrastructure Capacity</td>
<td>
■ Are the resources adequate to implement and sustain the changes?
■ What support will be required from the district office?
■ What support will be required from external technical assistance providers?
■ Has the team redefined role requirements?
■ Has the team updated processes, policies, procedures, and practices?
■ Has the team changed organization and communication structures to facilitate the changes?
■ Does the implementation plan outstrip the team's capacity to manage it? Should you start smaller?
</td>
</tr>
<tr>
<td>Communication and Buy-in</td>
<td>
■ Are as many stakeholders as reasonable employed in communicating the implementation process?
■ Are key stakeholders, particularly those who are resistant, meeting regularly to remain aligned with the implementation efforts?
■ Was the scope of the implementation plan designed to maximize buy-in?
■ Are there quick wins built into the plan that can be publicized to generate program support?
</td>
</tr>
<tr>
<td>Professional Development</td>
<td>
■ What specific capacity development has been initiated for critical groups, such as teachers and administrators?
■ What processes are in place to track ongoing skill-development requirements?
■ Has the team initiated an integrated and all-encompassing staff development plan?
</td>
</tr>
</table>

STAGE: Implement the Plan; Monitor and Adjust

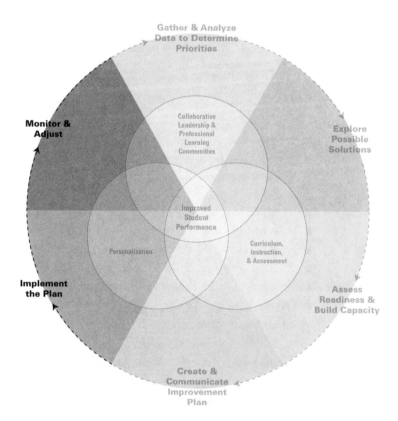

Here we cover the final two stages of the *Breaking Ranks* Process Circle: Implement the Plan and Monitor and Adjust. They are presented together because the minute that implementation starts, monitoring and preparing to make adjustments must begin. All of the team's hard work comes down to these stages. Although it's impossible to get everything right or to foresee all obstacles, the work done so far has prepared the team to move forward with conviction and confidence and to weather the inevitable challenges. It is time now for three things: support, support, and more support. The leader must be ready to take immediate action when things get out of tune (which they will) because people are not reading off the same sheet of music. Once you launch, don't be surprised to hear comments that span the whole gamut from negative to positive:

- This is a lot harder than I thought it would be.
- I know we got training on this, but I'm not sure this is really working for me.
- The students keep asking me if this is really necessary.
- I wish we'd had more time to prepare for this.
- I'm going to grieve this!
- Things feel out of sync.
- I'm worn out but really excited about what's happening!
- The students are nervous about the increased accountability, but they get it.
- The parents are coming around.
- I had a parent tell me her daughter really liked what we are doing.
- We are really focusing on the students for the first time.

Even top-performing individuals and teams may be nervous and a bit unsteady on their feet in the beginning, regardless of the professional development or training they have taken. New behaviors aren't smooth or comfortable at first. Think about the last time you took a lesson in a sport. It's typical after a lesson for your performance to get worse for a short time until the new behaviors are integrated into your overall game. You must be ready to make adjustments and provide support to help everyone find their game and bring it to a higher level.

Change Leadership Activities

Adjustments are to be expected and will be necessary to ensure sustainability. This is an exciting time, but vigilance is required because regression to old patterns and habits is very easy when things get uncomfortable. Some of the keys to success are:

- Conduct one or two communication blitzes just before implementation to ensure that everyone understands what's happening and why
- Establish a communication process (a weekly newsletter, for example) that keeps everyone informed of the progress on a regular basis
- Institute effective monitoring strategies the moment you implement
- Ensure that you are getting real-time feedback on new activities and their impact
- Identify and publicize quick wins
- Provide personal coaching and support to those who are most affected by the change
- Address backsliding the minute you see it
- Remain vigilant to infrastructure and policy changes that must be made to sustain the initiative
- Call on expert help
- Plan for an audit by an outsider to ensure that what the team or the school said it was doing is actually being done

Activities: Implement the Plan; Monitor and Adjust

The following matrix reflects those core change leadership elements and questions that surface during the Implement the Plan and Monitor and Adjust stages of the change process. Each section of the process circle has a similar matrix. *(The list below is a sample and is not intended to provide all of the information for any given initiative. Tailor it to your school's needs.)* The *BR* team should discuss and complete the activities matrix in each chapter. This exercise will help to ensure that your team has considered most areas related to the initiative. An example of a combined activity chart can be found in the schoolwide literacy initiative matrix on p. 100.

<table>
<tr>
<td rowspan="5">Essential Elements of Each Step</td>
<td>Sources of Data and Analysis</td>
<td>
■ Has the team identified all the relevant qualitative and quantitative measures necessary to track the implementation progress?
■ Are there methodologies in place to compile the data and to analyze it quickly so that course corrections can be made in a timely fashion?
■ Are data-collection and analysis roles clear or in need of adjustment?
■ What are the initial data telling you?
</td>
</tr>
<tr>
<td>Collaborative Leadership</td>
<td>
■ Is the team sharing leadership as adjustments to the implementation plan are made?
■ Now that you have data, does the team see any new leadership roles emerging as a result of your changes?
■ Students can play a key role in monitoring the implementation process and impact of change. How will you engage them as true partners in the process?
</td>
</tr>
<tr>
<td>Infrastructure Capacity</td>
<td>
■ Are the resources keeping up with the needs?
■ Have new resource needs been identified?
■ Are there any additional needs for changes in processes, policies, procedures, or practices?
■ Are any additional role refinements necessary?
■ Are any new roles required?
■ Are the changes stretching the staff in any ways that weren't predicted? What will you do if that is the case?
</td>
</tr>
<tr>
<td>Communication and Buy-In</td>
<td>
■ Are there any quick wins yet, and if so, have they been communicated?
■ Is the communication plan being kept current?
■ Is it effective, or does it need adjustment?
■ Are there any surprise reactions from stakeholders? If so, do they require any changes to the communication and buy-in plans?
</td>
</tr>
<tr>
<td>Professional Development</td>
<td>
■ Are the professional development activities keeping up with the changes?
■ Are the professional development activities being adjusted to meet unforeseen needs?
■ Are experiences with the changes being effectively incorporated into your professional development activities? Are lessons learned being leveraged appropriately?
</td>
</tr>
</table>

HOW?

Actual Initiatives Mapped to the Process Circle

So what might a *Breaking Ranks* Framework recommendation—or any initiative—look like mapped to the Process Circle? What would the different stages look like? Here are three different initiatives that follow the process circle stages:

■ Student-led conferencing

■ Literacy initiative

■ Advisories

You will note that each initiative is portrayed differently. Although the process circle provides a good visual, it can only contain limited information within it for presentation. The other two initiatives are portrayed in expanded prose. Although it is clearly important how you portray and communicate the stages, what matters most is that you are faithful in analyzing and following each stage of the process. One final note about these samples: they are single initiatives. Often you will have more than one initiative in progress and the plans may be considerably more complex.

Example: Student Led Conferencing

The following graphic maps the student-led conferencing initiative to the process circle. It offers an example of how your team might view this initiative from 30,000 feet.

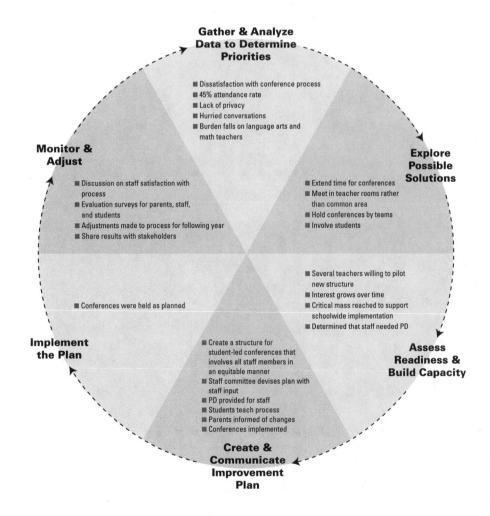

Example: Schoolwide Literacy Initiative

The following matrix maps the schoolwide literacy initiative to the process circle and offers an example of a combined activity chart.

	Gather and Analyze Data to Determine Priorities ▶	Explore Possible Solutions ▶	Assess Readiness and Build Capacity ▶	Create and Communicate Improvement Plan ▶	Implement the Plan ▶	Monitor and Adjust ▶
Sources of Data and Analysis	■ Diagnostic assessment ■ Reading test (SRI, SDRT, Gates) ■ Schoolwide ■ Annual ■ By grade equivalent ■ By lexile ■ Lexile all textbooks	■ *Breaking Ranks* ■ Culture of literacy ■ Double the work ■ ID preferred diagnostic assessment ■ Testing logistics ■ Feeder school principal	■ Diagnostic assessment by grade eq., stanine, and lexile	■ Match student data with lexile levels of textbooks. ■ Make data available to all teachers in electronic gradebook	■ Plan document including interventions, professional development, assessments, etc. ■ Data indicates widespread issues that exceed the capacity of this or any school to correct at once ■ Literacy coach to collect data	■ Program audit ■ Diagnostic assessment (annual) ■ Student progress in interventions (monthly)
Collaborative Leadership	■ Hire literacy coach ■ Form literacy council ■ Principal is part of the LC ■ District approval for diagnostic assessment	■ Identify tasks and ask literacy council members to volunteer ■ Literacy coach leads meetings	■ Literacy coach ■ Literacy council ■ Department chairs ■ "Skunkworks" team	■ Literacy council w/ literacy coach with principal as sitting member create plan	■ Literacy coach is the primary backed up by the literacy council ■ Principal's role is to remove barriers and to secure resources	■ Work with literacy coach takes on appearances of a partnership. Likewise, the literacy coach works collaboratively with the literacy council
Infrastructure Capacity	■ Review policies ■ Prepare budget for initial assessments	■ Literacy coach will need help in navigating various departments and teams with each having different needs and different readiness levels	■ Diagnostic assessment data will reveal extent of reading problem	■ Large numbers of students below grade level. Decisions will need to be made about whom to place in intervention classes	■ Identify staff members with knowledge in specific areas relative to the identified literacy strategies (vocabulary, graphic organizers, readalouds/thinkalouds ■ One hour per month of required professional development ■ New teachers receive intensified, yearlong training ■ Literacy coach is lead mentor	■ Need exceeds physical capacity ■ Vertical articulation grows in importance ■ Meetings held with all feeder school leaders

Communication and Buy-In	Professional Development
■ Literacy Council plans staff presentation ■ Newsletters ■ Staff meeting ■ ID driving and restraining forces, teachers on board v. those waiting = new teachers, non-tenured	■ PD survey to construct baseline of teachers' skills (needs assessment) ■ Literacy council conducts training w/ council members ■ Survey administrators to determine their readiness levels
■ Set up small meetings to discuss literacy approaches	■ Literacy council identifies schoolwide strategies ■ Literacy coach sets up training schedule
■ Mini-meetings reveal concerns of staff	■ Professional development plan (personal learning plans—PLPs)
■ Presentation to site council or leadership group	■ A core of strategies is identified for PD of all teachers ■ Content-specific needs are identified by the literacy coach and communicated to the literacy council
■ Feedback from site council ■ Modify presentation ■ Strategies identified ■ Training begins ■ Focus long-term ■ Don't force "laggards" or "late majority" ■ Skunkworks team uses experimental strategies ■ Send "innovators" and "early adopters" to outside training	■ Innovators and early adopters lead staff meetings under guidance of literacy coach
■ Staff meeting (presentation) ■ Interventions begin at mid-year with no resistance from staff or parents ■ Monthly training begun ■ New teachers on board	■ Professional development is planned a month in advance to keep pace with current issues and developments

Example: Advisory Implementation

This school chose to start advisories with incoming freshmen and have students remain with the same adviser for four years. Within four years all grades will have advisories in place. For the sake of brevity, timeframes and potential implementation derailers are not noted.

Steps Prior to Implementation Planning

1. The leadership team, through observation and a general review of student data, determines that more must be done to become student-centered and improve the level of personalization.

2. The principal with input from the leadership team creates a *BR* team with key stakeholder representation, to include potential resisters.

3. The *BR* team clarifies objectives, identifies and assigns key roles, creates a meeting protocol and schedule, creates an initial project plan, creates a charter, and confirms commitment of all team members.

4. The *BR* team conducts a communication and buy-in plan. Additional stakeholders may be added to the team at this time.

5. The *BR* team communicates its purpose and goal development process to key stakeholders—and invites participation on subteams as necessary (publicizing the team charter is usually part of this step).

6. The *BR* team does a data "drill down" to find ways to improve student outcomes and create a more personalized environment.

7. The *BR* team collects needs data directly from students and other stakeholders. Stakeholders are invited to participate in the data collection and needs analysis.

8. Based on data, the *BR* team confirms the need for a higher level of personalization, and sets two preliminary goals: teaming of teachers for freshman students and creating advisories.

9. The *BR* team communicates the findings of its data analysis to stakeholders.

10. The *BR* team conducts best practices research on teacher teaming and advisory programs to identify options. (Stakeholders are involved in this process, which includes visits to a half-dozen schools with successful mentoring and advisory programs.)

11. The *BR* team finalizes its goal and approach—to create an advisory program (but not to do teacher teaming for freshmen at this time)—and communicates this to all stakeholders.

12. The *BR* team considers seeking outside technical assistance in its quest to identify and define the five key elements of any effective program: purpose; organization (who, when, time, frequency, etc.); content (academic, social, etc.); assessment (impact, processes for course corrections, etc.); and leadership. Input from successful programs identified in the best practices research and school site visits is built into the program.

13. The *BR* team communicates the program design to stakeholders and makes revisions as necessary.

14. The *BR* team conducts readiness assessment and redesigns jobs (with stakeholders) that will be affected by the change. It identifies how the role of teachers and guidance counselors will change once advisories are implemented and includes the identification of any readiness gaps and required professional development.

15. The *BR* team communicates the results of the readiness assessment and needs for capacity building to stakeholders.
16. The union contract is modified to account for role changes.
17. Capacity building activities take place.

Implementation Planning

1. Tailor the implementation plan for presentation to stakeholders.
2. Update the communication plan for the advisory implementation process.
3. Present draft implementation plan (to include the communication plan) to stakeholders—revise as necessary.
4. Revisit the initiative mapping exercise to ensure that priorities for the whole school are clear, make sense, and are used to take unnecessary work off the plate for those affected by the changes.
5. Confirm that there are sufficient resources to carry out the program as designed.
6. Confirm or assign leaders for key elements of the advisory program, such as curriculum development, assessment (ongoing monitoring and adjustment), professional development training, and ongoing coaching.
7. Identify and line up internal (district) and external (TA provider) resources as necessary.
8. Continue readiness activities, such as infrastructure and leadership capacity building; role redefining; and modifying processes, policies, procedures, practices, and structures to support advisories. Design these changes to ensure program sustainability.
9. Adjust the schedule to accommodate four 25-minute advisory sessions a day immediately after the lunch period.
10. Create or purchase advisory content.
11. Orient teachers to the adviser role.
12. Conduct professional development advisory training (continuation of capacity building) for teachers and for those in program implementation leadership roles (see point 5 above). This includes role clarification and clear permission to discard behaviors and practices that are no longer required.
13. Add information on advisories to the orientation program for eighth graders and their parents, and conduct this orientation program.
14. Conduct advisory kick-off meetings for whole school.
15. Implement advisories.
16. Monitor and conduct debriefs (teacher and students) on a frequent and regular basis for the first three months and less frequently as the program gets its legs under it.
17. Provide additional professional development as needed.
18. Adjust advisory curriculum as required.
19. Communicate progress to whole community and describe successes.
20. Repeat cycle of activities above for next freshman class and new set of teachers moving into the adviser role.

Promoting Discussion Around "How"

How Do We Improve Our School?

In the award-winning 1957 film *Bridge over the River Kwai*, a British colonel rallies the spirit and morale of the Allied troops in a Japanese prisoner of war camp from the depths of despair by engaging them in the construction of a railroad bridge. Completing an excellent bridge by a deadline becomes a passion that motivates the prisoners to engage productively and almost happily. Just as the prisoners complete the task, Allied troops attack and begin to destroy their prized bridge, the purpose of which is to transport supplies to the enemy. This realization causes instant reflection for the prisoners on their real goal as Allied soldiers—to defeat the enemy. The bridge project changed the culture of the POW camp by providing morale-building activity for the troops; however, it was activity that was counter to the purpose of their very existence—their real culture.

- What is the real culture of your school? On whom or what is its focus?
- Programs to improve learning sometimes create activity that builds spirit and morale. How might you prevent an improvement initiative that seems like a good thing from becoming something that in reality has no positive impact on student learning?
- What beliefs do members of your school community hold that support the development of a culture that is student focused in every way?
- What beliefs do members of your school community hold that are counter to the development of a student-focused culture?
- How can your team maintain a focus on your mission so that you do not become so obsessed with the improvement plan or initiative that you lose sight of the outcomes?
- How will your team ensure that improvements resulting from your work will be sustained as a piece of a student-focused culture?
- How will your team ensure that engaging in each of the steps in the change process will contribute to securing the involvement and ownership of all members of your school community?

Who? CHAPTER 4

WHO? DO YOU AND YOUR TEAM HAVE WHAT IT TAKES TO CREATE A CULTURE FOR SCHOOL IMPROVEMENT?

Drucker wrote that "culture eats strategies for breakfast." It may seem unusual to include that quote in a book replete with strategies and recommendations for school improvement, but the school leader who neglects this wisdom imperils the implementation of even the most-tested best practices. How often have you heard it said that the culture of a school wouldn't allow an initiative to be implemented or that the personality of a leader wasn't right for a school? Your school culture must be prepared to support, adopt, adapt, and sustain a given initiative before it can be implemented. Does that mean that an initiative that your leadership team strongly supports should be abandoned simply because the culture does not support it? Not necessarily. Leadership takes many forms, not the least of which is helping to change or create a culture that will support significant improvement.

According to Seashore Louis and Wahlstrom (2011), "Organizations with stronger cultures are more adaptable, have higher member motivation and commitment, are more cooperative and better able to resolve conflicts, have greater capacity for innovation, and are more effective in achieving their goals" (p. 52). Adaptability, motivation, commitment, and cooperation are clearly attributes needed for innovation to thrive, but how can a principal or other leader encourage these? There are two ways in which leaders influence the all-important area of instruction: setting a tone that supports continual professional learning and taking "explicit steps to engage with individual teachers about their own growth." In addition, Seashore Louis and Wahlstrom (2011) found that three elements are necessary for a school culture that stimulates teachers to improve instruction:

- "First, teachers and administrators need to engage in deeper organizational learning—learning that uses all of the knowledge and resources that can be brought to bear on the core problems of practice in their particular setting" (p. 54).

- "Second, teachers need to be part of a professional community that breaks down the isolation and short term focus of the traditional school culture. Groups of teachers and their administrators focus on reflective inquiry and learning, with an explicit emphasis on how shared knowledge improves student learning" (p. 54).

- "Third, neither organizational learning nor professional community can endure without trust—between teachers and administrators, among teachers, and between teachers and parents" (p. 55).

Seashore Louis and Wahlstrom (2011) also found that those attributes are more prevalent at the elementary levels than in secondary schools. So how can middle and high school leaders emulate their successful elementary colleagues and better influence the cultures of their schools? By building trusting relationships and a professional learning community that engages all of the resources at their disposal, school leaders can have a profound impact on changing the mind-sets and dispositions within the school. To reiterate Dweck's point about mind-sets (see p. 6), what people believe about success drives their behavior. The beliefs of leaders within your classrooms and within your school matter. Do you and other staff members in your school have high expectations for yourselves as well as the students? If leaders believe that leadership is innate and therefore they cannot grow as leaders, can the culture improve? Time, work, and deliberate practice can result in success for individuals and your improvement efforts!

The "who" of the *Breaking Ranks* Framework begins with a look in the mirror. Outside factors may be obstacles to changing the culture, but your own practices and attitudes—and the practices of every leader in your school—may also hinder culture shift. The idea for comprehensive school improvement may not begin in the principal's office, but it most assuredly can end there as a result of incomplete planning, failure to involve others, neglect, or failure to create conditions so that things can change. Creating those conditions is often the first challenge—and sometimes it must start with the principal's own thinking and interactions with people. Usually when the status quo is found wanting, our initial impulse is to seek to change the world around us. Students, parents, teachers, school boards, districts, communities, states, and even the nation too often think, "If only *X* were different—then everything would be fine." As you begin to think about change, keep this thought in mind as you interact with others: *I cannot change you—I can only change how I respond to you.*

Fortunately, leadership practices and the capacity to foster the trust, motivation, commitment, and cooperation necessary to implement improvement initiatives can be learned. Collaborative leadership requires a high degree of personal awareness by you and every leader within your school—administrator, teacher, or student. This chapter should be used to help you and every leader within your school increase the positive daily influences you can have on culture. Chapter 3 focused on how process and fidelity of implementation can similarly affect the school's culture and the success of initiatives.

Assessment and Professional Development: Learning to Lead

Often professional development revolves around increasing knowledge and changing convictions, yet most collaboration breaks down because of inexperience and limited skills or behaviors, rather than a lack of knowledge or conviction and motivation. Schools must understand that the consideration of the "what" and "how" of school reform is not sufficient for success. The personal capacity of the people involved in leading the school improvement efforts—the "who"—is also essential to successful improvement.

How often do you, as a school leader, look at your own behavior or look to develop leadership skills in teacher leaders and the leadership team? Too often, school leaders pull a group together for a meeting and call it collaboration. But genuine collaboration happens because of the school leaders' skills and behaviors. What skills, knowledge, and beliefs do the participants bring to the table?

WHO?

Q: Why would a seasoned principal or assistant principal with a lot of classroom experience need to assess his or her strengths and weaknesses?

A: Every school leader needs to know his or her strengths and areas of challenge. By nature, many people who have become principals are confident in their abilities. The reality, however, is that most school leaders and aspiring leaders are strong in one or two areas and they lead with those strengths—sometimes exclusively with those strengths. Unfortunately, they may rely on those strengths for everything.

A strength that is overused becomes a weakness. For example, one principal's strength might be sensitivity. The principal always has the pulse of what's going on and the staff loves him or her—until the principal relies exclusively on sensitivity, and judgment and decisiveness take a backseat.

Another common example is the principal who is very decisive. Decisions are made quickly and firmly, but the decisions may be weak because of a lack of analysis, data, or evidence and without sensitive regard for those who will be affected by the decision. Quick decisions are not necessarily good decisions. This kind of principal makes lots of decisions with bad results, which leads to a loss of effectiveness that in turn affects the school culture. The idea of practicing leadership skills is to ensure a proper balance in the integration of different skills to create the best result.

Culture can be changed and leadership skills can be developed. NASSP has engaged in the observation, assessment, and development of professional skills to help thousands of school leaders become more effective. That experience has demonstrated that regardless of where a school leader is in his or her career, it's appropriate to engage in a skills assessment and development process that is designed to enhance effective performance. Further, because effective leadership practice is crucially important to school reform, principals and other school leaders must encourage aspiring leaders and staff members to examine and develop their own professional capacity. By doing so, educators grow personally even as they sustain improvements in their schools. Too often, principals share best practices with colleagues in terms of programs and approaches to leading, but never get around to reflecting on and discussing the personal elements of their success or their strengths and weaknesses—which more often than not are the very things that enabled a best practice to be successfully adopted.

Too Busy to Lead?

The demands on school leaders at all levels are daunting—even a cursory review of what principals undertake in an average emergency-free week is instructive. But if you are too busy to regularly undertake the type of practice and reflection required to be effective in the areas of educational leadership, resolving complex problems, communication, and developing self and others, then you are too busy to lead.

Think about why you became a teacher, an assistant principal, or a principal. Was it to be a disciplinarian, to help the buses run on time, to chair meetings? Probably not. Compare what you do on a daily basis with what you would *like to do* to improve student learning. Are you leading with purpose or allowing daily activities to dictate your personal trajectory—and as a consequence, the trajectory of your school. Without recommitting to your personal mission and continuous self-assessment, you may wake up 30 years into your career and wonder why. Complete the following exercise, and it should soon become clear why it may be time to change your practice.

Things I Do	Things I Should Do But Don't Have Time	How I Resolve to Address or Things I Shouldn't Do

The benefits of effective and efficient school leadership:

- fosters improved learning
- prepares leaders in ways formal preparation course work did not
- helps leaders model behavior for every professional in the school
- builds capacity for school initiatives
- frees up time through efficient practices

The goal of this section is to help each school leader—principal, assistant principal, teacher leader, or other staff member—begin to assess his or her knowledge, skills, and dispositions for leading change by examining and practicing 10 leadership skills. Only by doing so can a leader be prepared to take the "what" and the "how" of school improvement and put them into effective practice so that all students learn and grow. At the heart of any school improvement initiative is a focus on individual development for every member of your team. The same process can guide the analysis and assessment of leaders' needs and strengths. The principal should be the model and driving force behind administrator and teacher self- and peer-assessment and development.

Collectively the 10 leadership skills identified by NASSP are referred to as the "NASSP 21st Century Principal Skills" (See figure 4.1). The skills are also aligned with the *Educational Leadership Policy Standards: ISLLC 2008*.

Figure 4.1

21st Century Principal Skills

Educational Leadership

- **Setting instructional direction.** Implementing strategies for improving teaching and learning, including putting programs and improvement efforts into action. Developing a vision of learning and establishing clear goals; providing direction in achieving stated goals; encouraging others to contribute to goal achievement; securing commitment to a course of action from individuals and groups.
- **Teamwork.** Seeking and encouraging the involvement of team members. Modeling and encouraging the behaviors that move the group to task completion. Supporting group accomplishment.
- **Sensitivity.** Perceiving the needs and concerns of others; dealing tactfully with others in emotionally stressful situations or in conflict. Knowing what information to communicate and to whom. Relating to people of varying ethnic, cultural, and religious backgrounds.

Resolving Complex Problems

- **Judgment.** Ability to make high-quality decisions that are based on data; skill in identifying educational needs and setting priorities; assigning appropriate priority to issues; and in exercising caution. Ability to seek, analyze, and interpret relevant data.
- **Results orientation.** Assuming responsibility. Recognizing when a decision is required. Taking prompt action on the basis of data as issues emerge. Resolving short-term issues while balancing them against long-term objectives.
- **Organizational ability.** Planning and scheduling one's own work and the work of others so that resources are used appropriately. Scheduling flow of activities; establishing procedures to monitor projects. Practicing time and task management; knowing what to delegate and to whom.

Communication

- **Oral communication.** Communicating clearly. Making oral presentations that are succinct and easy to understand.
- **Written communication.** Ability to express ideas clearly and correctly in writing; to write appropriately for different audiences—students, teachers, parents, and others.

Developing Self and Others

- **Developing others.** Teaching, coaching, and helping others. Providing specific feedback that is based on observations and data.
- **Understanding own strengths and weaknesses.** Identifying personal strengths and weaknesses. Taking responsibility for improvement by actively pursuing developmental activities. Striving for continuous learning.

You might look at the skills and say "Oh, that's easy" or "I am effective in all of those categories." In truth, there is very little that is earth-shattering about the skills. Yet time and again, people who simply understand the general skills too rarely integrate them into their practice. They rely on just a couple of the skills. Further, if they took the time to ask their peers to assess them on these "simple" skills, the peers might offer a very different perspective.

Q: What happens when a school leader doesn't examine his or her own strengths and weaknesses?

A: Unconscious incompetence. It may sound harsh, but that's the reality. It is possible, but highly unlikely, that a principal can be good in all these skills without extensive awareness and practice. Unfortunately, that could mean muddling along (unconsciously) with a level of competence veiled in good intentions that does nothing to improve student learning within the school. More concretely, schools in which leaders don't set the instructional direction have everyone doing their own thing with haphazard results; where teamwork is missing, hierarchical top-down decision making takes place; where sensitivity reins supreme at the expense of other skills, the principal is always running around trying to make up for bad decisions; where judgment and analysis are lacking, the principal shoots from the hip; where the principal has not made a concerted effort to develop others, a sense of dependency takes over and the staff can't function when the principal leaves the building—even for the day. The skills for leadership require a complex balancing act—one that takes practice and motivation. If you don't have the right motivation, then the skills don't matter: you have to believe in people and have a sincere desire to move things forward.

The skill dimensions are component parts of the broader task of effective school leadership. It is important that school leaders find opportunities for practice and feedback in each of these areas. Before selecting areas of focus for professional development, however, school leaders and aspiring leaders must first assess their strengths. Too often educators use the "deficit model" to guide their development. But participants in NASSP skills assessments focus on their areas of strength first to reinforce the idea that school leaders should practice and build on strengths rather than only focus on improving weaknesses.

Certainly there are weaknesses that can derail your career; however, most weaknesses can be eliminated or managed with proper and sustained development through collaboration with others who have strengths in your areas of weakness. This can only occur with accurate self-knowledge and application of specific strategies to diminish the effect of the weaknesses on professional performance. Know your strengths and build upon them to ameliorate some of your deficits.

How Are Skills and Behavior Related?

Skill manifests itself through behavior—usually complex behavior appropriately applied in the context of a specific situation. Each of the skill dimensions relies on demonstrations of specific behaviors for diagnosis of strength or weakness and for further development. Specific behavioral indicators further define each skill dimension. Each skill dimension has its own unique descriptors of practice. For example, a leader skilled in setting instructional direction would exhibit the following behaviors:

- Articulates a vision related to teaching and learning
- Articulates high performance expectations for self or others

- Encourages improvement in teaching and learning
- Sets clear, measurable objectives
- Generates enthusiasm toward common goals
- Seeks to develop alliances outside the school to support high-quality teaching and learning
- Acknowledges achievement or accomplishments
- Seeks commitment to a course of action.

The indicators provide actions that can be practiced and refined. A colleague or a coach can observe them and provide specific feedback regarding the level of effectiveness demonstrated during practice and performance. Behavioral indicators can become the focus of purposeful and intentional practice in the context of the job setting. Without indicators or descriptors, it becomes difficult if not impossible to gauge one's effectiveness.

NASSP has developed a process for school improvement and skill development that you can use to focus your efforts. The process includes six components:

- Gather and Analyze Data to Determine Priorities
- Explore Possible Solutions
- Assess Readiness and Build Capacity
- Create and Communicate Improvement Plan
- Implement the Plan
- Monitor and Adjust (return to Gather and Analyze Data)

Knowledge: What one knows.
Skills: What one can do. How are knowledge and skills related? Aeronautical engineers probably know a great deal more about *how* planes fly than pilots know. But would you rather fly with an experienced pilot or an aeronautical engineer?
Dispositions: Who one is and what one believes (includes personal traits and characteristics).
Habits: Behaviors that result from repeated and successful use of behavioral indicators associated with skills.

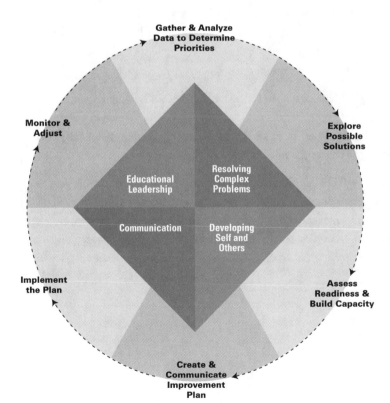

Gather & Analyze Data to Determine Priorities

Monitor & Adjust

Explore Possible Solutions

Educational Leadership

Resolving Complex Problems

Communication

Developing Self and Others

Implement the Plan

Assess Readiness & Build Capacity

Create & Communicate Improvement Plan

The process circle as it relates to school improvement was discussed in greater detail in Chapter 3; however, the process circle should be used for more than school improvement. Every leader in your school should use the same process to develop a cohesive plan for self-improvement. The self-assessment tools offered in the following pages will help you understand your leadership strengths and weaknesses so that you can implement the *Breaking Ranks* Framework; however, they are only a first step in improving your leadership capacity. These tools and worksheets should be used by every leader in your school.

NASSP offers an online assessment tool at www.nassp.org/lsa. The online version of the NASSP Leadership Skills Assessment includes five steps:

1. Exploration of the skills dimensions. You will examine your interest in developing specific skills that have proven to be essential to effective school leadership.

2. A 360-degree skills assessment. You will assess your own practice of these same skills and invite up to 15 colleagues to assess your practice so that you may compare how others perceive your performance with your own perceptions. The purpose of the 360-degree tool is to help determine the behaviors you exhibit as a part of your typical response to most situations you deal with. When people are under pressure, they resort to the behaviors or habits that have served them well, that have gotten them where they are. When you consider the frequency with which you engage in each of the behaviors in the assessment, think of the habits and the behaviors that are most frequently part of your initial response to situations. Note: All responses are confidential.

3. In-basket activity. Your responses to a variety of issues that school leaders typically face will be used to assess your performance in the skill dimensions during the in-basket activity. You may assess your own performance and have the opportunity to request that two colleagues assess your performance as demonstrated in your in-basket responses.

4. Reports. When you complete the activities described above, you may view and print a report for each. When you have completed all of the assessment activities, you may view and print a summary report that pulls together data from all three of these sources. This report ranks the skills in terms of your developmental interests and level of skill demonstrated.

5. Development plan. After reviewing the data in your summary report, you will decide which skills you want to develop first and which types of professional development strategies work best for you. The final report will provide you with specific developmental strategies and a development guide for building an individualized personal learning plan that are based on those decisions.

WHO?

Reflect on Your Current Practice in Each of the Skill Dimensions

NASSP's *10 Skills for Successful School Leaders* offers additional, more-detailed tools for self-assessment, feedback, mentoring, and coaching. Although the self-assessment component is extremely important, your perception of your strengths and weaknesses is only one piece of the puzzle. As a starting point, complete the activities on the following pages to better understand your perception of your current practices in each of the 10 skill areas (activities on pp 113–120). These will help you to complete the Gather and Analyze Data section of the process circle. You will then explore other areas of the process circle, and how to use mentorships and feedback to guide your development efforts and practice behaviors when addressing real school-related issues. (see pp. 122)

Activity #1: How Do *You* Put It in Action?

To begin to self-assess your capacity in **setting instructional direction**, reflect on what it looks like when you perform each of the behaviors. List some specific examples from your own practice as evidence that you can and do perform each behavior.

Personal Reflection: My View	
Behavior/descriptor	**Give examples of your performance of this behavior and the frequency with which it occurs. Be specific.**
Articulates a vision related to teaching and learning	
Articulates high performance expectations for self and others	
Encourages improvement in teaching and learning	
Sets clear, measurable objectives	
Generates enthusiasm toward common goals	
Seeks to develop alliances outside the school to support high-quality teaching and learning	
Acknowledges achievement and accomplishments	
Seeks commitment to a course of action	

To begin to self-assess your capacity in **teamwork**, reflect on what it looks like when you perform each of the behaviors. List some specific examples from your own practice as evidence that you can and do perform this behavior.

Personal Reflection: My View	
Behavior/descriptor	**Give examples of your performance of this behavior and the frequency with which it occurs. Be specific.**
Supports the ideas of team members	
Encourages team members to share ideas	
Contributes ideas for accomplishing the team's goals	
Assists in performing the operational tasks of the team	
Seeks input from team members	
Acts to maintain direction or focus to achieve the team's goals	
Seeks consensus among team members	

To begin to self-assess your capacity in **sensitivity**, reflect on what it looks like when you perform each of the behaviors. List some specific examples from your own practice that could serve as evidence that you can and do perform this behavior.

Personal Reflection: My View

Behavior/descriptor	Give examples of your performance of this behavior and the frequency with which it occurs. Be specific.
Interacts professionally and tactfully with others	
Elicits perceptions, feelings, and concerns of others	
Voices disagreement without creating unnecessary conflict	
Communicates necessary information to appropriate persons in a timely manner	
Expresses written, verbal, and nonverbal recognition of feelings, needs, and concerns in responding to others	

To begin to self-assess your capacity in **judgment**, reflect on what it looks like when you perform each of the behaviors. List some specific examples from your own practice as evidence that you can and do perform each behavior.

Personal Reflection: My View	
Behavior/descriptor	**Give examples of your performance of this behavior and the frequency with which it occurs. Be specific.**
Takes action within the bounds of appropriate priority	
Acts with caution when approaching an unfamiliar person or situation	
Analyzes information to determine the important elements of a situation	
Communicates a clear rationale for a decision	
Seeks additional information	
Uses information sources that are relevant to an issue	
Asks follow-up questions to clarify information	
Seeks to identify the cause of a problem	
Sees relationships among issues	

WH02

To begin to self-assess your capacity in **results orientation**, reflect on what it looks like when you perform each of the behaviors. List some specific examples from your own practice as evidence that you can and do perform each behavior.

Personal Reflection: My View	
Behavior/descriptor	**Give examples of your performance of this behavior and the frequency with which it occurs. Be specific.**
Takes action to move issues toward closure	
Initiates action for improvement	
Determines the criteria that indicate a problem or an issue is resolved	
Considers the implications of a decision before taking action	
Makes decisions on the basis of information	
Relates individual issues to the larger picture	

WHO?

To begin to self-assess your capacity in **organizational ability**, reflect on what it looks like when you perform each of the behaviors. List some specific examples from your own practice as evidence that you can and do perform this behavior.

Personal Reflection: My View	
Behavior/descriptor	**Give examples of your performance of this behavior and the frequency with which it occurs. Be specific.**
Delegates responsibilities to others	
Plans to monitor delegated responsibilities	
Develops action plans	
Monitors progress	
Establishes timelines, schedules, and milestones	
Prepares for meetings	
Uses available resources	

WHO?

To begin to self-assess your capacity in **oral communication**, reflect on what it looks like when you perform each of the behaviors. List some specific examples from your own practice that serve as evidence that you can and do perform this behavior.

Personal Reflection: My View	
Behavior/descriptor	**Give examples of your performance of this behavior and the frequency with which it occurs. Be specific.**
Demonstrates effective presentation skills	
Speaks articulately	
Uses proper grammar, pronunciation, diction, and syntax	
Tailors messages to meet the needs of unique audiences	
Clearly presents thoughts and ideas in one-on-one, small-group, and formal presentation settings	
Uses available resources	

WHO?

To begin to self-assess your capacity in **written communication**, reflect on what it looks like when you perform each of the behaviors. List some specific examples from your own practice as evidence that you can and do perform each behavior.

Personal Reflection: My View	
Behavior/descriptor	**Give examples of your performance of this behavior and the frequency with which it occurs. Be specific.**
Writes concisely	
Demonstrates technical proficiency in writing	
Expresses ideas clearly in writing	
Writes appropriately for different audiences	

WHO?

To begin to self-assess your capacity in **developing others**, reflect on what it looks like when you perform each of the behaviors. List some specific examples from your own practice as evidence that you can and do perform each behavior.

Personal Reflection: My View	
Behavior/descriptor	**Give examples of your performance of this behavior and the frequency with which it occurs. Be specific.**
Shares expertise gained through experience	
Encourages others to change behaviors that inhibit professional growth	
Recommends specific developmental strategies	
Asks others for their perceptions of their professional development needs	
Seeks agreement on specific actions to be taken for developmental growth	

To begin to self assess your capacity in **understanding your own strengths and weaknesses**, reflect on what it looks like when you perform each of the behaviors. List some specific examples from your own practice as evidence that you can and do perform this behavior.

Personal Reflection: My View	
Behavior/descriptor	**Give examples of your performance of this behavior and the frequency with which it occurs. Be specific.**
Recognizes own strengths	
Recognizes own developmental needs	

Activity #2: Get Feedback on Your Current Practice in Each of the Skill Dimensions

The 10 self-assessment exercises you have just completed are important first steps in understanding your perceptions of your skills. Knowing the skills—and the perceptions others have of your skills—can help you integrate them into practice.

This activity is designed to help you complete a very similar exercise but through the eyes of a mentor, supervisor, or a colleague. (**Setting instructional direction** is the only component included here. For the other skill dimensions, see *10 Skills for Successful School Leaders*, available through www.nassp.org.)

Discuss the skill **setting instructional direction** and its indicators with your supervisor, mentor, or coach. Elicit feedback regarding your effectiveness in demonstrating these skills. Discuss strategies for practice that builds greater capacity.

Feedback: View of a Colleague, Supervisor, Mentor, or Coach		
Behavior/descriptor	**Effectiveness in demonstrating**	**Strategies to build capacity**
Articulates a vision related to teaching and learning		
Articulates high performance expectations for self or others		
Encourages improvement in teaching and learning		
Sets clear, measurable objectives		
Generates enthusiasm toward common goals		
Seeks to develop alliances outside the school to support high-quality teaching and learning		
Acknowledges achievement and accomplishments		
Seeks commitment to a course of action		

WHO?

Activity #3: Complete a Component of the Process Circle

With Activities 1 and 2, the self-assessment and the mentor assessment exercises, completed, let's revisit the process circle to discover your next activity for growth.

- Gather and Analyze Data to Determine Priorities
- Explore Possible Solutions
- Assess Readiness and Build Capacity
- Create and Communicate Improvement Plan
- Implement the Plan
- Monitor and Adjust (return to Gather and Analyze Data)

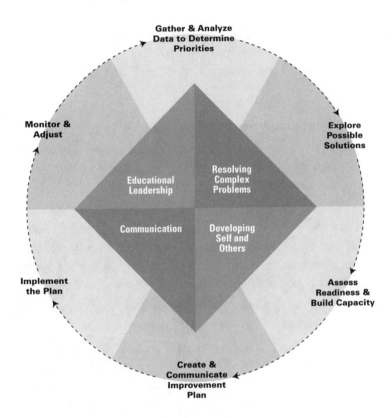

In *10 Skills for Successful School Leaders*, worksheets are provided for each of the 10 skills along with the six-step process for each. For example, the principal or other school leader is asked to complete each component of the process circle as it relates to one of the skill dimensions. (A completed example related to the skill dimension Setting Instructional Direction follows.) To understand the data required for each, the principal or other leader would need to keep in mind the descriptors of practice and behaviors for Setting Instructional Direction:

- Articulates a vision related to teaching and learning
- Articulates high performance expectations for self or others
- Encourages improvement in teaching and learning
- Sets clear, measurable objectives
- Generates enthusiasm toward common goals
- Seeks to develop alliances outside the school to support high-quality teaching and learning
- Acknowledges achievement or accomplishments
- Seeks commitment to a course of action.

Gather and Analyze Data	**Ask: How is my on-the-job performance in this skill area?** ■ Reflect on my performance of the setting instructional direction behavioral indicators—the frequency of my engaging in each behavior as opposed to my ability to perform the behavior. ■ Solicit face-to-face feedback from a variety of sources—such as a mentor, a coach, a supervisor, supervisees, and colleagues—that focuses on the setting instructional direction indicators. ■ Seek anonymous feedback from the 360-degree tool available from NASSP (www.principals.org). ■ Seek data from a formal assessment process (e.g., Selecting and Developing 21st Century Leaders or Leadership Skills Assessments from NASSP). ■ Review how I measure my performance on the indicators. Discuss results with mentor or colleague.
Possible Solutions and Strategies	**Assignments that stretch and provide practice in this skill** ■ Accept leadership of an ad hoc group with a difficult task, a group of inexperienced or unskilled people, or a loosely structured group to practice bringing structure and direction to a group in order to accomplish tasks. ■ Convene a committee or task force to study an issue regarding teaching and learning. Use a written charge that you have drafted for that group. In that charge, include the specific purpose and objectives for the group related to improved learning, the advisory or decision-making status of the group, resources that are available to assist in the group's work, to whom the group will report, your expectations, and deadlines or a timeline. ■ Meet regularly with staff members to discuss their priorities. Provide input on the basis of your expectations as an instructional leader in the organization. ■ Study group dynamics in actual work groups and identify the behaviors that assist and hinder the groups in completing their tasks. ■ Seek opportunities to chair problem-solving committees at the school or district level. Ask a mentor or a colleague to monitor progress and provide feedback regarding effective use of planning skills and follow-through. ■ Organize your faculty into focus groups. Form a cadre to train aspiring leaders within your own school or district and lead this group yourself. **Workshops, seminars, and courses** ■ Check your district, regional service agency, state department, or colleges and universities in your area for opportunities for building capacity in this skill area. ■ Participate in seminars dealing with effective management or administration or how to conduct effective meetings. **Mentor, coaches, and supervisors** ■ Develop a mentor relationship with a colleague who can provide guidance in identifying critical instructional leadership and school management issues and in assigning appropriate priority to these issues.

WHO?

Process Circle Step	How Do *You* Put the Skill Into Action? Example: Setting instructional direction
Possible Solutions and Strategies	■ Discuss with a mentor actual school issues focusing on the effective school leader's use of skills in judgment and results orientation to set high priorities for instructional leadership and the management of learning. **Readings** ■ Bennis, W. (2009) *On becoming a leader: The leadership classic.* (Rev. ed.) Philadelphia, PA: Basic Books, ■ Blanchard, K., Carew, D., & Parisi-Carew, E. (2009). *The one minute manager builds high performing teams: Excellence through team building.* New York, NY: William Morrow,. ■ Blasé, J. J., & Kirby, P. C. (2000). *Bringing out the best in teachers: What effective principals do.* (2nd ed.) Thousand Oaks, CA: Corwin Press, ■ Carnegie, D., & Associates, Inc. (2001). *The leader in you: How to win friends, influence people, and succeed in a changing world.* New York, NY: Simon & Schuster. **Off-the-job development opportunities** ■ Become active in community and professional organizations. Seek leadership roles within committees in these organizations. ■ Participate in a district-level or state-level seminar or graduate course in group dynamics or interpersonal communications. **NASSP professional development opportunities** ■ Online courses ■ Seminars ■ Web-based resources ■ Customized professional development (Visit www.principals.org/ProfessionalDevelopment.aspx to see current offerings.)
Assess Readiness and Build Capacity	■ Review the possible solutions in light of school data that has implications for my professional development needs: achievement; instructional staff members' qualifications, experience, background, and so on; student, staff member, and school community demographics; attendance; drop-out rate; graduation rate; and so on. ■ Ask: What development can I engage in that will have the greatest impact on my personal/ professional capacity and the needs of the school? ■ Consider how specific personal development activities will affect others with whom you work.
Create and Communicate Plan	■ Develop a personal learning plan (PLP) that delineates how you will practice this skill, your development activities, and your goals. (See Chapter 7 to create a PLP.) ■ Be an example of a "head learner" by sharing your PLP with others and encouraging every adult in the building to have a learning plan that is based on their developmental needs in the context of the needs of the school and the students.
Implement Plan	■ Practice the indicators to build capacity in the skill: implement the strategies selected from possible solutions.

WHO?

Process Circle Step	How Do *You* Put the Skill Into Action? Example: Setting instructional direction
Monitor and Adjust	■ Take continual measures of your progress and the impact of your progress on the needs of your school as you practice.
	■ Refer to the data sources you used in collecting the original data that formed the basis of your development plan (PLP).
	■ Seek feedback from colleagues, peers, mentors, and supervisors—and remember the PLP is public!
	■ Reflect.
	■ Keep a journal.
	■ Return to Gather and Analyze Data to establish new priorities with the same skill or to begin work on another skill.

To reinforce the point that assessment and development should be a continual process, you will note that the last bullet instructs the leader to return to the Gather and Analyze Data step to establish new priorities either within the same skill or to begin work on another skill. Improvement is incremental and therefore requires you to continually adjust and reset your priorities and goals on the basis of monitoring. Sometimes that will mean that you are satisfied that your practice in a skill is just enough to get you where you want to be for the moment and instead need to address another skill. At other times, monitoring may point you in the direction of continuing to practice certain behaviors or to set new priorities within the same skill.

You should now complete this process for each of the 10 skill areas. (See *10 Skills for Succesful School Leaders.*) Once you have completed the process, you will realize that the following developmental components appear repeatedly:

- Mentoring, coaching, and reflection
- Simulations and practice
- Feedback.

A mentor can have a profound impact on your leadership—regardless of the stage of your career. While confiding professional weaknesses to mentors may seem risky, the relationship between a mentor and a protégé must be a trusting one. As you continue to revisit your strengths and weaknesses, you should expect your mentor to engage in some of the following activities:

- Observing your behavior in specific situations as requested by you
- Listening to your analysis of your concerns and behaviors as they relate to the skills and knowledge you seek to develop
- Giving you specific feedback about your behavior
- Reinforcing your effective performances and achievements with behaviorally specific feedback
- Helping you explore strategies for building on the strengths you consistently demonstrate
- Helping you explore strategies for refining performances and behaviors that are not as effective as you would like

Mentoring

A *mentor* is an experienced role model who guides the professional development of a less-experienced protégé through coaching. Both the mentor and the protégé learn about themselves, improve their skills, and grow professionally. Coaching involves the skills of observing and recording behavior, giving feedback, asking probing questions that enhance reflection, listening, analyzing behavior as it relates to professional skill, and acquiring knowledge.

WHO?

- Sharing with you his or her understanding of education organization structures and cultures
- Introducing you to other experienced administrators who might serve as mentors to you in their own areas of expertise and experience.

Simulations: The Art of Practice

Other than a fire drill, when was the last time you simulated handling a work-related issue involving peers? Much of the skills assessment work done by NASSP revolves around simulations of school-related activities. Those activities not only help in the selection of school leaders but also are extremely beneficial in helping experienced principals understand their strengths and weaknesses.

Simulations are so effective because they:

- Provide a low-threat environment in which to practice and learn the process for on-the-job development of specific skills
- Provide structured opportunities for learning the skills and indicators more fully
- Remove the possibility of negative ramifications for mistakes and errors in judgment made during practice
- Remove emotional ties that may be attached to real-life situations
- Create opportunities for receiving immediate feedback about performance and effectiveness from observers
- Open opportunities for dialogue that is not fettered by confidentiality concerns that may exist around real-life situations.

There are a number of simulations provided in *10 Skills for Successful School Leaders* as well as detailed protocols for how to engage in the simulations. However, to help you understand the types of simulations in which school leaders should regularly engage, a sample scenario follows. (See Appendix 5 for an article about aligning professional development with school needs.) A scenario typically requires a "performer," at least one "responder," and at least one "observer." The content of these learning and practice activities gives participants opportunities to practice specific behavioral indicators as well as to become familiar with realistic situations that they will, in all probability, encounter as they serve as school leaders.

Beyond Simulation

The school provides a laboratory for improving leadership capacity. You don't have to create a simulation. Real-life events present opportunities to learn and grow. Most school leaders say that they got to be as good as they are by learning from real-life experiences on the job!

WHO?

Sample Scenario
Teacher Evaluation—Northeast Middle School

As principal of Northeast Middle School, you are concerned about the teacher evaluation procedure that is being used at the school. A conversation with science teacher Leslie Hines reinforced your worry. Leslie was referred to you for some alleged deficiencies. You were concerned about how best to evaluate Leslie for both summative and formative purposes. You found the present system to be of no help.

You have decided to form a committee of Northeast faculty members to help you start from scratch in formulating an evaluation procedure to effectively diagnose teachers' strengths and identify areas for improvement. You are interested in a system that can be used to determine whether a teacher is to be given tenure, but the major thrust of any exceptional system is to help teachers grow professionally. Observation instruments are needed to support the evaluation procedure.

A committee—composed of your assistant principal, a guidance counselor, the teachers association building representative, and two team leaders—is meeting with you after school in the conference room to talk about a new evaluation process that ultimately will be used to advise the district level evaluation committee.

Conduct the meeting.

The Feedback Loop

Once the simulation has concluded, feedback begins. Feedback is a powerful tool for growth and development. Key elements of the feedback include:

- Observer facilitates.
- The performer reflects on his or her performance and states three examples of effective performance and one thing that he or she would do differently.
- The responder provides feedback regarding three effective demonstrations of skill and makes one suggestion for improved performance. The feedback should focus first on the skills selected by the performer. They may also include skills from other areas if they were particularly strong or particularly weak.
- The observer gives feedback to fill in the blanks using the notes made during the performance to substantiate. The observer might note, for example, that when the performer said, "I need to know what you think and how you feel about this issue," it was a strong example of the sensitivity indicator, eliciting the feelings, needs, and concerns of others.

Keep the ratio of three positives to one suggestion. Frequently, the performer will start with the things that he or she did not perform well. Stop them by saying, "Time out. Start with the things you believe you did well." Try to give as much time to each of the behaviors performed well as to the behavior not performed well.

Feedback is a gift. When we receive it, we should say only, "Thank you." There is no need for the performer to justify, explain, rationalize, or defend behavior or performance. This takes time and is not productive.

The gift of feedback should generate reflection. The recipient should "try it on" to see how it fits. As with other gifts, some will be more valuable than others. Honestly reflecting on the feedback to determine its value is an important step in using the information to guide efforts to improve performance.

WHO?

Reflection

Beyond simulations, actual events within your school are also good opportunities for growth. When a mentor cannot observe your behavior or performance firsthand, reflective review and coaching are used. This approach requires that you record and analyze your own behavior for improved performance. In a meeting with you after the event or incident, your mentor can assist you in further analysis of your performance and work with you to explore ways to improve. The key skills used by the mentor in this coaching activity are listening, questioning, and being sensitive. An effective mentor will help you explore options and reach your own decisions about courses of action that best fit your situation.

Use the following questions as a reflection guide to record and analyze your performance in preparation for a conversation with your mentor. Outline the situation you want to analyze, and write responses considering the following prompts:

- The basic nature of the situation
- How and why the situation developed
- The primary issues and concerns—yours and those of others
- Your objectives and strategy
- The critical verbal and nonverbal behavior of people involved in the situation, including your own behavior (what has been said and done)
- The outcomes to date
- Your overall reaction to the situation
- What you have done well
- What you will do differently another time
- What you have learned from the situation.

(You may send your mentor a copy of your reflections prior to the meeting.)

Q: What is a distinguishing benefit of assessment?

A: Feedback. School leaders can sometimes become numb to praise, criticism, and blame and the regular struggle of who to listen to on any given topic. A genuine and thoughtful assessment process is an opportunity for growth, rather than an evaluation process or other exchanges that have an opportunity to become adversarial.

If you want to become a better leader, external feedback is critical. You have to understand how you measure up against certain skill sets—not only in your own eyes but also in the eyes of others. You can't develop yourself unless you're aware of how others see you.

Visualize the Johari window—a four-pane window, with each pane representing a different view: the traits that the participant and peers see (arena); the things that the participant sees but the peers do not (façade); the things that the peers see but the participant does not (blind spot), and the behaviors or motives that were not ascribed to the participant by anyone. It is important to understand and appreciate the importance of each of these panes or perspectives. Developing a systematic process to gather those perspectives will ensure the most favorable results. The more organized your feedback process and the wider the net you cast for feedback, the more potential there is for professional growth.

Source: Luft, J., & Ingham, H. (1955). The Johari window, a graphic model of interpersonal awareness. *Proceedings of the Western Training Laboratory in Group Development.* Los Angeles, CA: University of California–Los Angeles.

Johari Window

	Known to Self	Unknown to Self
Known to Others	My Public Self (arena)	My Blind Spots
Unknown to Others	My Hidden Self (façade)	My Unconscious Self

WHO?

Creating Your Personal Learning Plan

Successful leaders know themselves. Self-knowledge comes from seeking feedback from others, reflecting on what you are doing, being honest with yourself, and not letting success go to your head. Using the tools provided in the preceding pages as well as in *10 Skills for School Leaders* and other resources, create a written personal learning plan for your own development. The important factors in your development plan will be your ability to learn from your experiences and observations.

Using your self-assessment data, personal reflection, the feedback from peers involved in simulations, and your mentor, you should be able to identify behaviors and skills that require your attention. Consider the skill dimensions that have emerged as high-priority areas of development for you. Your developmental priorities should be based on your own strengths and weaknesses as well as the needs of your school. Ask yourself, What do I need to develop in myself to be a better leader while meeting the needs of my school?

For example, if setting instructional direction is a weakness for you, then improving instruction in your school will only happen if you strengthen that set of skills. Start with one skill and focus your efforts on building your capacity in that skill as you engage in improving your school. Be sure to list a skill dimension and the behavioral indicators you want to develop.

Skill Dimension:

Identify opportunities within your present job responsibilities or seek out special activities and projects that will allow you to focus on your development objectives. Consider the ways you can:

- Tap the expertise of experienced administrators in education and other fields
- Locate relevant reference material
- Participate in professional courses, seminars, and workshops
- Affiliate with professional organizations
- Serve in field assignments, such as internships
- Fill in for an administrator who is on leave
- Organize special projects within the school, the district, or the community.

Ask yourself:

- What will I do to build my capacity?
- Who will be involved or affected?
- When and where will it be done?
- How will it be monitored and who will provide feedback regarding your progress or performance?
- How does it relate to the school improvement plan?

Be specific when answering these questions. The more detailed your plan is, the easier it will be to follow the plan and to accomplish your goals for professional growth. Whether it be a journal or other method, be sure to engage in reflection. Set aside 15 minutes at the end of each day to reflect on your development plan as it relates to the events of the day.

Journal

Keeping a journal helps you maintain your developmental focus and fosters effective reflection on your experiences. Ask yourself if you learned anything from an assignment, a supervisor, a challenge, a development activity, or an off-the-job experience. Ask yourself, What did I do well or not so well? What will I do the same or differently next time? Capture those ideas in your journal.

Use the journal to record a situation or an event, the skill and behavioral indicator you used, and how it affected your skill development. Then note your reflections. The journal ties all your learning experiences together. Writing in your journal—putting your feelings and perceptions into words—can be a powerful tool for learning. The journal will also help you share your experiences with a mentor or colleague. To make the most effective use of the mentor in reflecting upon a given situation, details matter!

WHO?

"Who" Can Make or Break the "What"

In this chapter, the importance of leadership to and in the culture has been a focal point. Unfortunately, too many school leaders in the past interpreted leadership as residing within one office or as only being shared among a few key stakeholders. The "who" of leadership within this chapter and within this book refers to teacher leaders, student leaders, team leaders, the leadership team, the assistant principal, and the principal. Each of those leaders would be well served to engage in the activities, self-assessment, reflection, and professional development contained in this book. The principal can, of course, be a leader in modeling these activities. Without key leaders who understand their individual skills, strengths, and weaknesses, culture is very difficult to change, which makes implementing the "what" of the *Breaking Ranks* Framework very difficult indeed.

Promoting Discussion Around "Who"
Who? Do You and Your Team Have What It Takes?

It has often been said that the only way to improve schools is to improve the capacity of people who work in them. The people who make up the school community—the who—are certainly a critical component of any change effort. As you consider that component, use the following questions as conversation starters to raise awareness of important considerations and to prepare to assess readiness and build capacity necessary for success:

- Change does not happen without resistance. From whom does your team anticipate the greatest resistance? What are the reasons for it? How can you engage school community members early in the process to reduce resistance? How can you use the success of early adopters in reducing resistance in others?

- How will your team assess the readiness of everyone involved in the change without creating unnecessary conflict? How will you assess all aspects of the school, including support staff members' roles, teaching, and administrative practices, to determine if current practices and structures support or hinder success? How will you assess the attitudes of community members toward the initiative as it relates to their attitudes toward their current practice?

- Once you determine readiness, how will your team provide resources, time, support, and structures to build readiness to levels required for success? How will you determine and clearly communicate the roles of school community members to maximize their contributions to the effort? What current roles need to change? How will your team build the knowledge and skills required by new role requirements?

- What other initiatives are currently ongoing in your school? How will you adjust the priorities of your team to foster attainment of your improvement goals? What are you willing to stop doing or combine with other initiatives to support reaching your goals?

Profiles in Progress

Each year the MetLife Foundation–NASSP Breakthrough Schools program identifies and showcases high-achieving and dramatically improving schools that serve large numbers of students who live in poverty. High poverty rates add a layer of complexity to the challenges that many schools face, yet the Breakthrough Schools have demonstrated that *complex* and *insurmountable* are not interchangeable terms. In fact, it is the added level of complexity that has caused the leaders and staff members of some of the Breakthrough Schools to embrace a more cohesive culture so that they could collaboratively adapt strategies to improve achievement and allow students to thrive.

To see how schools focus on the core areas of collaborative leadership; personalizing the school environment; and curriculum, instruction, and assessment, three Breakthrough Schools—one K–8 school, one middle school, and one high school—agreed to be featured in the following pages. Although your circumstances may differ significantly from the three profiled schools, the underlying lessons and areas of focus are applicable to all schools interested in improvement.

Douglas Taylor School

Chicago, IL ■ www.taylor.cps.k12.il.us

Principal: William Truesdale

Community: Urban

Grades: PreK–8

Enrollment: 730

Demographic:

Hispanic 87%

Black/African American 10%

White.. 3%

Free and reduced-priced meals 97.1%

Mobility rate.. 20%

2009 METLIFE FOUNDATION–NASSP BREAKTHROUGH SCHOOL

Rooted in Community

Inspiring students to become teachers and community leaders is a goal of Douglas Taylor School's leadership team. Continuity and connection are important to the school, which opened in the 19th century. Housed in a beautiful old school building in Chicago's South Side, Taylor contains grades preK–8. To maintain the feeling and benefits of the middle school model, the middle school students take classes in an annex outside the main building. Despite this separation, the students are surrounded by something that feels greater than themselves—an institution that has been part of the community since 1878, when Taylor was built for approximately $2,000.

The main hallway is lined with graduation photographs that document changes in the population from the early German and Swedish students to more recent Hispanic and Black/African American students. A more contemporary account of the importance of the school to the community and vice versa can be told by seven current teachers who were students at Taylor. The school was and remains an important fixture to the residents—one they wish to support and protect.

Staff members reach out to the community through such events as Family Math Night, Family Literacy Night, and Taylor Family Fun Fair, each of which attracts more than 400 students, parents, members of the local East Side Chamber of Commerce, the ward alderman, and other community members. Parents reciprocate by supporting the school in many ways, including the parent patrol, a unique group of 35 parents who help ensure the safety and well-being of the students during arrival and dismissal times. In May 2008, Mayor Richard M. Daley recognized the Taylor Parent Patrol at his annual safety luncheon as one of the best parent patrols in the Chicago Public Schools. During the day, parents also provide additional help in the school as greeters in the main entranceway.

Parents commend the school for its structure and clear rules, and they appreciate its discipline and emphasis on safety. They also commend the teachers for their willingness to work with the students and to listen to parents' concerns. Principal William Truesdale believes that the supportive environment created at the school, coupled with a cooperative home-school community link, is the surest formula for sustaining interest in lifelong learning.

Serving approximately 752 students, Taylor is large but not overcrowded. Because Taylor is considered a high-achieving school, it is eligible to receive students from underachieving schools, but its location on the far south side of Chicago means that few take advantage of this opportunity. Ninety-seven percent of its students are eligible for free or reduced-price meals. The school's rigorous, project-based curriculum is aligned with the Illinois Learning Standards and provides opportunities to students in the surrounding community.

Collaborative Leadership

During his six-year tenure, Truesdale has promoted rigor by building a common vision that all students can achieve outstanding academic excellence in the core subject areas: reading, mathematics, science, and social studies. His hope is to create an environment that encourages the maximum intellectual, emotional, physical, and social growth of each individual. Taylor's eight-member instructional leadership team—five teachers representing both general education and special education, two administrators, and the counselor/case manager—helps articulate and maintain that vision and create an environment of maximum learning.

Vertical academic and schoolwide comprehensive planning committees and horizontal grade-level and department-level committees support effective schoolwide planning by serving as the structures by which all faculty members can offer input. Teachers also share best practices, review student data, and solve student problems in weekly grade-level meetings. Staff members have established professional learning communities using the School Teams Achieving Results for Students (STARS) program model, which has improved the level of collaboration. "The STARS program helped me develop strong bonds with my staff," said Truesdale. Teachers can also sign up to host staff meetings in their classrooms to profile ideas on teaching and learning. Teachers who attend these meetings take a "My Best Ideas" sheet into other teachers' classrooms to record best practices.

Staff members believe that Taylor's emphasis on cooperative learning and sharing has taken root because of those structured collaborative times and the Friday cross-grade professional development days. "Schools need to be safe, diverse, creative, and democratic environments that inspire and adapt to the changing needs of students, teachers, parents, and the community," said Truesdale, referring to the importance of collegiality and collaboration. The teaching teams systematically foster that creativity and adaptability within the school; therefore, allowing them the freedom to inspire students is essential. "When [the] teachers are happy and treated as professionals, that's when we make AYP," Truesdale said.

Systems have also been created to involve parents through the No Child Left Behind parent committee and the bilingual advisory committee, both of which advise the leadership team and share community concerns. All communications are distributed in English and Spanish to reach as many parents as possible. Moreover, the school offers ESL classes to its parents through a partnership with Olive Harvey College, and parents can participate in computer training. Truesdale is also plugged into the community and he has been commended for his active participation on many local committees that support the community. Past and present community collaboration spawned a twice-a-month mentoring and tutoring program that is sponsored by the Eastside Chamber of Commerce, and an art program sponsored by Chicago Communities in the Schools is held twice a week.

"The *Breaking Ranks* Framework is extremely valuable to urban schools," noted Truesdale. "The challenges of urban schools' high poverty, gang influences, and other factors present an opportunity for teachers, staff, and parents to collaborate to solve problems. I have been able to help influence and develop my parents at Taylor School to become leaders. My LSC [Legal Services Corporation] chairperson was able to get the school community to get over 800 signatures to have a camera placed on a corner where there was illegal neighborhood activity going on that was affecting the school community. The collaborative efforts of this LSC chairperson to get everybody to work together to ensure the safety of the children was acknowledged by the Chicago police."

Collaboration takes place regularly within the school walls as well. At the K–5 level, the school has academic learning committees in reading, language arts, social studies, and science—and the teachers choose their committees. In addition, grade levels meet during a common planning time to share best instructional practices, student data, and Scantron assessments, and teachers in grades 2–8 plan lessons together. On the basis of the assessment results, the teachers can provide more individual, differentiated, and group instruction. The school is also focusing on improving vocabulary instruction and read-aloud strategies schoolwide from K–8. The Taylor instructional leadership team—which is composed of teachers from the primary, intermediate, and middle schools—is collaborating and giving performance-management sessions on key insights, such as using vocabulary skills—particularly context clues—and broader exposure to new vocabulary to improve reading comprehension scores. The team developed an action plan in six areas, including professional development in reading vocabulary strategies and schoolwide daily "read-alouds."

Personalizing Your School Environment
"Urban schools face more challenges of poverty and possible single parents and grandparents raising children," said Truesdale. "The role of the teacher has become one of a mentor, a role model of possibility. Many students do not have positive role models and face many challenging situations at home. The school becomes a beacon of light and a place of security." Truesdale said that to 93% of students report having supportive teachers and staff members as step in the right direction.

Building personal connections between students and others in the school or between students and their learning becomes difficult when poor discipline is an issue. School leaders recognized that students' behavior had become an issue at Taylor and that the current discipline system was not meeting the needs of the students, the staff members, or the school. The staff rejected the well-worn path of using punitive measures that remove students from classrooms and prevent teachers from teaching. Instead, they implemented a positive discipline plan and calm classroom that focuses on meeting students' social and emotional needs.

During the first three days of school, students learn about classroom expectations—be respectful, be responsible, and be your best—and the expectations matrix. At the heart of the initiative are teacher-created, consistent discipline plans; class rules; and consequences and incentives for positive behavior intervention. Quarterly events reinforce the positive behavior.

Taylor offers robust in- and after-school programs to address individual students' interests and needs. These include:

- The After School Academic Program, which is held four days a week from 2:30 p.m. to 4:30 p.m. for both remediation and enrichment.
- Getting Us Ready for Life (GURL), a 15-week program for seventh-grade girls that teaches self-esteem, conflict resolution, career education, and financial planning (done in conjunction with Chicago Communities in Schools)
- All Stars Program, a 13-week research-based, interactive drug-prevention program for

seventh-grade boys that focuses on future goals, personal commitment, and community ties, but does not directly talk about drugs

- The Power to Change, a 12-week program in which selected students in grades 5–8 meet in a peer-to-peer setting to learn impulse control and anger management techniques
- A peer-tutoring program in which eighth graders work with third graders to improve their academic performance—a potential boon to mentors and protégés.

Such programs are reminders of how the little things can make a big difference in school environments and to academic success. According to teacher Bernice Zambrano, this principle applies to English language learning. "Students are identified and tested for English fluency as soon as possible after enrollment," she said. "The general education teachers collaborate with the bilingual staff to best address the needs of those students [who] do not have an instructor that speaks the native language." Zambrano also reports that "the culture of our ELL students and their families is validated and respected in many programs and activities throughout the school year. These projects give students the opportunity to learn and grow by using both their Spanish and English skills in all the content areas, including the arts."

Teachers try to make strong connections with students by offering extra tutoring time in the morning, and every teacher is also involved in the schoolwide Universal Breakfast Program, in which students pick up their hot or cold breakfast and join the teachers for breakfast in their individual classrooms before the school day begins.

Curriculum, Instruction, and Assessment

One reason that Taylor continues to have high test scores is because teachers spend time on data analysis. Grade-level and individual plans are developed for the students and the overall school. Each teacher receives a data chart and data binder showing how his or her students are performing by indicator. Because the teachers have been trained to make data-driven decisions, they are able to focus their strategies on very specific areas—and seek out the resources they need.

Those resources or insights may come from as close as the classroom next door or through a more formal professional development program. "Next door" insights are gathered through peer walk-throughs, the STARS program, common planning time, and interaction with the school's literacy coach. On Friday mornings, before the students start the day, teachers participate in more formal professional development to learn new strategies and benchmarking information in both reading and math.

Staff members are always looking for ways to increase the degree to which students are challenged—especially in the areas of math and literacy. The school increased the amount of vocabulary development strategies and read-aloud instruction across all grades in an effort to fulfill the school's mission statement, which states: "All Taylor students will become confident, capable readers, who will read for pleasure and knowledge for the rest of their lives."

Thanks to a grant, students can now take algebra if they meet certain criteria and sign a contract agreeing to come to class every day and complete extra homework. As part of the grant, teacher Elinor Sullivan was able to receive special summer training and is paired with a coach who observes Sullivan's classroom every two weeks and identifies what is currently working and what is not. Each month, Sullivan and her coach and five other local grant recipients get together to share strategies and difficulties with teaching various concepts.

Sullivan said that in addition to those meetings, all the teachers in the school system who use the same textbooks get together monthly. "At these meetings, we gain a deeper understanding of the mathematics ourselves so that we can better teach our students," she said. "We have demonstrations of the lessons in the book, and two professors from the University of Chicago provide an in-depth look at the mathematics." Helping students pursue challenging next steps is a driving force behind choosing professional development, teaching strategies, and technology at Taylor. The emphasis on encouraging students to strive for entrance into Chicago's selective high schools pushes teachers to find ways to differentiate instruction for students who want more challenge. The faculty and the administrators regularly review the data to evaluate how students are measuring up to the challenges. Data sources include teacher assessments; Scantron fall, winter, and spring assessments; criterion-referenced tests, portfolios, analyses of strengths and weaknesses that were found during state testing, learning assessments in reading and math, and five-week progress reports.

Preparation for a smooth transition of Taylor students into high school includes:

- A career options education program. In this program eighth-grade students receive 40 minutes of career instruction once a week and the counselor/case manager speaks to the eighth-grade students about career choices and brings in guest speakers to help students gain a greater understanding of careers and the education required to enter them.

- High school investigation day, which includes a scavenger hunt at the local high school.

- Data analysis of Freshmen on Track to Graduate. In three years, they have seen growth from 43% of the students being on track to 81%. "We are setting new goals of moving that target up to 100%," said Truesdale. "We think this significant gain has come because of an emphasis on raising our standards of instruction in the classroom; collaborative leadership; personalizing the school environment; and curriculum, instruction, assessment, and technology that prepares our eighth-grade students to compete in a global economy. We have also noticed an increase in the number of eighth-grade students who have been accepted into select-enrollment schools in Chicago and have received scholarships."

Conclusion

Taylor has shown steady growth in student achievement during the last several years. Much of this can be attributed to the leadership of the principal and his staff. "I believe in lifelong learning as an instructional leader and head learner, striving each day to build a collective vision with students, teachers, parents, and the community of outstanding academic excellence," said Truesdale, noting the positive changes he has seen in the school's culture and levels of personalization and professional learning. Truesdale's vision has begun to pay such dividends as improved composite reading, mathematics, and science scores on state standards tests. Together with consistent professional development, the use of student achievement data for instructional decisions, and parent involvement, Taylor's focus is where it belongs: promoting exceptional student performance.

Pocomoke Middle School

Pocomoke City, MD ■ www.pocomokemiddle.org

Principal: Caroline Bloxom

Community: Rural

Grades: 4–8

Enrollment: 460

Demographics:

White	48%
Black/African American	43%
Asian	2%
Other	2%
Free or reduced-price lunch	61%
Reading on grade level	83%

2008 METLIFE FOUNDATION–NASSP BREAKTHROUGH SCHOOL

Pride Is the First Step

When visitors step inside Pocomoke Middle School in Pocomoke City, MD, they are immediately surrounded by a profound sense of pride, caring, and high expectations. Beanbag chairs await eager readers, a fish pond offers a quiet place, and comfortable chairs and tables provide space for mentors to help students. As you walk through the building, students are actively engaged in instruction, the classroom walls are covered with student work, and the halls are lined with inspiring quotes and pictures of students demonstrating success.

Students are celebrated every day at Pocomoke. Two students of the day are recognized during live morning announcements. Readers, writers, mathematicians, geographers, and scientists are selected monthly, and a formal recognition assembly is held quarterly for each grade level. In its quest to make learning personal, Pocomoke designs each initiative to "put a face on the data," said Principal Caroline Bloxom. "It's our job to figure out what each student needs. It's the job of the team to own their children and their children's achievement."

Pocomoke is located at the very southern end of Maryland's Eastern Shore and serves a diverse population, with 61% of students qualifying for the free or reduced-priced meals program and 10% receiving special education services. The school is unique in that it runs both an elementary program and a middle school program under the same roof. Students enter Pocomoke as wide-eyed nine-year-olds and leave as preteens.

Pocomoke's school district, Worcester County Public Schools, provides considerable human and material resources to support the school's academic program. The school, with its commitment to shared leadership and partnerships with the community, has leveraged those resources into a comprehensive program that supports the complete development of each student. Noting the importance of continued support and diligence, Superintendent Jon Andes told a local newspaper, "Success is never an end-all. Public education is a continuous pursuit—an endless process, with new challenges and new opportunities around every corner."

Collaborative Leadership

Bloxom has assembled a dedicated staff of 59 professional educators and 24 support personnel. She is proud of the teamwork that has helped foster personnel stability since her first year as principal, when she was faced with hiring 14 teachers to fill vacancies. Whereas only 2% of the nation's 4.8 million teachers are Black/African American, 22% of Pocomoke's classroom teachers are minorities, creating a positive and dynamic environment that is a model of diversity.

Bloxom has nurtured shared decision making and established an extensive teaming structure. This structure aligns with the district's effort to enhance accountability in all of its schools and to use the Middle States Association of Colleges and Schools' Accreditation for Growth protocol to organize school improvement efforts. The teams include:

- The tri-school (elementary, middle, and high) Pocomoke Strategic Planning Council (PSPC) that includes administrators, professional and support staff members, parents, students, a county commissioner, a city councilman, a board of education member, a pastor, the Pocomoke mayor, the chamber of commerce director, the Pocomoke Library branch manager, an assistant superintendent, and several members of the business community

- A school-level Accreditation for Growth (AFG) team that includes administrators, staff members, parents, students, a district coordinator, a retired middle school teacher, and a former middle school student who is enrolled in a local college

- Specialized implementation teams that involve all staff members and focus on the areas of reading, math, arts immersion, achievement according to minority status and sex, school climate, character education, technology, and parent involvement

- Grade-level and special-area teams

- A school improvement advisory committee, as well as a PTA, that includes parents and teachers

- A ministers' gathering, whose membership includes pastors from the churches in Pocomoke.

The responsibility of the AFG team is to provide leadership to the implementation teams and to supervise the key steps in the school improvement planning process: analyzing data; identifying strengths and weaknesses; and creating, implementing, and monitoring action plans. The AFG team reviews what is happening at PSPC, implementation, and grade-level team meetings. Each AFG team meeting ends with a celebration of good news reported by team members. Key educators serve on more than one team. The principal is a participant on the AFG team, the school improvement committee, the PTA executive committee, and the ministers' gathering; she also chairs the PSPC. Implementation team chairs are members of the AFG team and the strategic planning council. Grade-level team leaders serve on the AFG team and one of the implementation teams. This crossover of members forms a communication link allowing concerns and suggestions to be carried back and forth between groups. Communication between the three Pocomoke schools occurs during the PSPC, internal coordinator, and regional principal meetings and opportunities during which staff members at the schools work together on projects, such as student transitions, and shared initiatives, such as the positive behavioral interventions and supports program.

Collaborative leadership at Pocomoke does not just involve adults. Students gain leadership skills by serving as representatives on the implementation teams and on the student faculty advisory board, as well as by participating in clubs and the annual grade-level service learning projects and community partnerships. Eighth-grade students who are interested in a possible teaching career can become involved in the teacher cadet program, where they form a bond with current teachers and discover the importance of working together. Staff members have made a concerted effort to encourage minority students to participate in the cadet program.

Collaboration at the classroom level is also quite strong and is supported by a district teacher mentoring program for first- and second-year teachers, coupled with targeted professional development. Pocomoke has adopted the use of instructional coaches who have been trained at the Salisbury University Academy for Leadership in education. As a result, the school's two instructional coaches, as well as the curriculum planner, are now able to analyze teacher needs, model classroom lessons, informally observe classes and provide oral and written feedback, collaborate with teachers on interventions, and provide some interventions directly to students.

School-community connections are a priority for Pocomoke. Bloxom and other staff members understand the importance of the larger community supporting the messages conveyed in the school. Consequently, the school has working relationships with the YMCA, the Salvation Army, local museums, and various community civic groups and government agencies.

Personalizing Your School Environment

Pocomoke staff members are committed to family and community involvement in their quest to improve each student's learning. For several years, parents have had access to up-to-date information on their children's progress through the PowerSchool/PowerGrade student data system and the homework hotline. To share information and encourage a spirit of community and pride, the school also schedules numerous parent and community activities each year, including family activities during each parent-teacher conference night, an intergenerational reading program, a multicultural fair, parent and grandparent lunch days, the Dads and Sons Dinner and a Movie, the Moms and Daughters Jewelry Jamboree, poetry slams, ice cream socials, the Black History Night of Celebration, family honors nights, Math Night, Tech Fest, the science fair, Technology Night, and the field day/art expo. Fourth-grade students take a walking tour of Pocomoke visiting the town's museums, theater, the Discovery Center, and city hall.

But family activities to address individual students' needs are only the beginning. Staff members know that a school without support for at-risk students—or "at-promise" as the staff refers to these students—is like a hospital without a trauma center. First, staff members have to be well trained. Some staff development, such as diversity training, is mandatory for all teachers. Staff development at the district and school level is based on a menu of research-based strategies, and other development, such as diversity training, is mandatory for all teachers.

Second, every student who does not experience success in the classroom has an individualized plan for success that is monitored weekly. These plans delineate the level of assistance that students require both in and out of the classroom. In addition, students can participate in the highly acclaimed after-school Pocomoke Pride Academies; 86% of students currently participate in the intervention and enrichment activities that these academies offer. Transportation is provided free of charge. "The academies address the whole child," said Jane Chisholm, the extended school administrator. "The academies change quarterly and cover a large spectrum of activities. Recent academies included homework assistance, skill remediation, robotics, Girl Scouts, violin and guitar lessons, Girls Growing Gracefully Club, glee, dance, basketball, Gentleman's Club, drama, and family workshops."

Third, the needs of the whole child are addressed. In addition to offering mentoring by staff members, eighth-grade cadets and high school students, the school invites successful Black/African American business leaders to speak to small groups of students. Meanwhile student wellness is emphasized through a partnership with the county health department in which a health counselor meets with students during the school day. Further, the district supplies a staff member to work with families in need of support in their homes; a behavior consultant to conduct functional behavior assessments and work with teams to develop behavior intervention plans for individual students; and a family connections facilitator to maintain a productive line of communication with families, make referrals for school and community services, and discuss home-learning activities the families can employ.

Pocomoke adopted the University of Oregon's positive behavioral interventions and supports program, which uses schoolwide rules, behavior lessons, and rewards. At the end of the school year, the coveted "peace flag" is given to the grade with the fewest disciplinary referrals during an afternoon of fun activities. "The behavioral program mirrors the academic efforts in that specific, individualized, data-based plans are designed for students who demonstrate behaviors of concern," said Assistant Principal Bryan Perry.

Positive messages go well beyond the realm of discipline, however. All students are encouraged to attend college, and each student participates in career planning each year. Fifth-grade students engage in career activities, complete a profile, and participate in Maryland Day at The University of Maryland–College Park; sixth-grade students participate in career cluster activities, play a career-oriented game, participate in a career fair at a local hospital, and visit the local community college; and seventh- and eighth-grade students participate in a career day, complete a five-year plan that outlines their activities during four years of high school and the year after they graduate, and visit the two local universities. During individual academic conferences with students, Bloxom has the opportunity to reinforce the importance of planning and achieving today, rather than waiting until it becomes much more difficult.

Curriculum, Instruction, and Assessment

Pocomoke has a cohesive curriculum structure that emphasizes math and literacy, with access to rigorous course work for all students. The school offers:

- One hundred fifty minutes of daily reading instruction
- Ninety minutes of daily math instruction
- Pre-algebra or Algebra I for all students in grade 7
- Algebra I or Algebra II for all students in grade 8
- High school French for all students in grades 6, 7, and 8
- High school Spanish for all students in grades 6, 7, and 8
- Arts immersion in all classes.

To support a challenging curriculum for all students, the instructional team (i.e., the principal, the assistant principals, the curriculum planner, and two instructional coaches) ensures quality instruction and delivery of the curriculum. The arts immersion specialist, along with the principal and more than half of the teachers, who have been specially trained in incorporating the arts into the curriculum, provide the guidance for seamless blending of the content and skills of art forms with those of cocurricular subjects. The results of these efforts are easy to evaluate because students create portfolios of their work and their work is displayed everywhere in the building.

Assessment and data use are also an area of strength for Pocomoke. "We are continuously evaluating what works," Bloxom said. "We are not afraid to make changes. Our whole mind-set is that we change teacher behavior to impact student achievement. Most of us played Pin the Tail on the Donkey at least once or twice as a child. You are blindfolded, turned around and around, and sent heading toward an unseen target. Sometimes luck is with you; sometimes it is not. That is teaching in the old days. Today, successful educators continuously collect, organize, and analyze data throughout the school year."

Individual student work is collected and examined across content areas during grade-level team meetings. The instructional team uses walk-throughs to monitor school norms and examine student products, and the team collects and examines content-area "vertical slices" on a regular basis. For example, a day is selected to collect student work in math from fourth-, fifth-, sixth-, seventh-, and eighth-grade classrooms. The work is examined to ensure that the level of rigor has increased from one grade to the next.

After each district benchmark assessment in the various content areas, teachers and the instructional team use a Web-based assessment platform to analyze each student's results by indicator. This software helps teachers differentiate instruction and provide necessary interventions to meet the needs of each child. Teachers and the instructional team regularly share data with individual students; administrators also meet with students individually to discuss their current grades and results of benchmark assessments. All data is organized by the instructional team into longitudinal studies by cohorts, tracking students over the five years of their middle school experience.

Pride Yields Achievement

One of Bloxom's first priorities upon coming to Pocomoke was to improve the way that people think about the school. "Pride is an essential precondition to learning: pride in the sense of a child's feeling of self-worth; pride from an understanding that staff members genuinely care about them; and pride in having a place to learn that is safe, orderly, and attractive," said Bloxom.

Before becoming principal in 2000, Bloxom had seen the school through the eyes of a middle class community member, a parent, a math teacher, a curriculum planner, and a district supervisor. She had a sense of what the actively involved stakeholders wanted the school to be, but she also knew that there were invisible stakeholders, those who were poor and too often preoccupied with more-pressing life issues, such as being a single parent, working to pay the rent and put food on the table, and worrying about a lack of adequate health insurance and violence and drugs in their neighborhoods. Those invisible stakeholders love their children, but they are not involved in their children's education on a consistent basis. On their behalf, Bloxom adopted a school vision of No Throw-Away Kids—a vision that the school would advocate for all children and would fill any gaps a child might have that a parent was unable to fill. Eleven years later, that vision is realized each day through the dedication and commitment of the school family, who have come to regard the potential failure of any student as unacceptable. The staff uses the kid friendly theme, "Respect + Responsibility = Pocomoke Pride!" on a daily basis to reinforce the academic and behavioral expectations they have for their students. Every staff member knows that true school improvement is a journey, not a destination.

Forest Grove High School

Forest Grove, OR ■ www.fgsd.k12.or.us

Principal: Karen Robinson

Community: Suburban/Urban fringe

Grades: 9–12

Enrollment: 1,977

Demographics:

White...61%

Hispanic 36%

Asian 1%

Black/African American 1%

Other... 1%

Free and reduced-price lunch.................. 42%

2008 METLIFE FOUNDATION–NASSP BREAKTHROUGH SCHOOL

A World of Opportunity

From the moment you enter the lobby, it is clear that Forest Grove (OR) High School places a high value on achievement for all students. Large banners highlight the recognition the school has received for academic accomplishments—such as Oregon's Closing the Achievement Gap award, which it has received for five out of the last six years—and for meeting adequate yearly progress.

In the classrooms, students are actively engaged in the subject matter, whether it is music, art, or history; a reading workshop for struggling readers; a class for English language learners; or an honors biology class that is open to all students.

The school's mission statement—"To provide a superior education that challenges our students to achieve academic and personal excellence and to become world-class citizens"—is posted throughout the school. And the statement is not an empty feel-good slogan. According to one student, "Our mission statement is what we really do; kids who come here go out of here ready for the world."

Expectations for student achievement are set high—and they are met or exceeded because of the school's personalized learning environment. As Dave Willard, the assistant superintendent for the Forest Grove School District, stated, "We set the bar high for every student and make the entire curriculum so that every student has access. The students know what is expected of them, and more important, they know we are committed to helping them succeed at the highest level. We have embraced the new three Rs of education for the 21st century: rigor, relevance, and relationships."

A transition in principalship occurred in August 2010, and the school improvement efforts have continued seamlessly because of a variety of factors. First, a 13-year veteran assistant principal, Karen Robinson, who served for the past six years at Forest Grove, was appointed principal. This was essential in carrying on the school improvement efforts because the previous principal, John O'Neill, believed strongly in a shared leadership structure that delegated responsibilities on the basis of administrative interests and skills. Each assistant principal was directly responsible for assigned school improvement initiatives, which allowed for rapid advancement on several fronts. Second, communication among members of the site administrative team occurred daily, and discussions centered on improvement initiatives and how to best address potential challenges through ongoing collaborative discussions. Third, structures put into place to ensure ongoing practice continued.

A major component of Forest Grove's success comes through the use of professional learning communities (PLCs) in which teacher leaders discuss their work and identify best instructional practices through data-driven decision making. Lastly, the former principal now serves as the district's director of student achievement with the assigned responsibility of supporting the replication of this school's success districtwide. Although he is available as a mentor for the new principal, he is not involved in the sustained improvement efforts that have led to continued levels of unprecedented success for the school.

Collaborative Leadership

Unless expectations are clearly articulated and measurable, they become aspirations, rather than expectations. To ensure that practice and instruction are driven by data, rather than anecdote, every two years Forest Grove holds a school improvement retreat during which representatives from all stakeholder groups (including teachers, students, parents, board members, and community members) review disaggregated student achievement data to examine program efficacy, the alignment of the curriculum to state standards, state graduation requirements, and professional development. They then establish school improvement goals for the next three to five years. Using data to drive professional development has also prompted the use of differentiated instruction, student-owned strategies, *Breaking Ranks II* recommendations, power standards (i.e., essential, prioritized standards), and other best practices.

In addition to traditional parent conference nights and quarterly Latino parent nights, Forest Grove offers parents a variety of tools and information to support high expectations. Parents use a Web-based service that provides biweekly updates and course expectations for each class and allows parents to check grades, missing assignments, assignment due dates, and attendance records. Forest Grove staff members also work closely with one another and with parents to support early intervention for struggling students. During weekly team meetings, teachers review individual student progress and, as a result, often initiate individual parent conferences to identify and implement intervention strategies. PLCs meet biweekly during late start time on Wednesdays for teacher collaboration and ongoing professional development. All teachers who share a common course serve on a course-specific PLC. During this time, teachers review student performance data and identify best instructional practices to improve initial instruction. Assistant principals provide a further check by coordinating student progress meetings for students who are failing multiple classes.

In the area of school-community connections, the staff reports an atmosphere of support consistent with the district's goal of increasing community awareness of the Search Institute's 40 Developmental Assets (available at www.search-institute.org/assets). The developmental assets are experiences and qualities that students should have to become successful, caring, responsible adults. The school's message about supporting youth is spread in local churches and shared with service clubs and business groups. The results are manifested in the school when business leaders conduct mock interviews with all sophomores as part of the job-shadowing advisory requirement and when community and business leaders serve as mentors for senior projects, are guest speakers for classes, and critique résumés.

Personalizing Your School Environment

Forest Grove is continually striving to meet the needs of each student and has embraced a host of strategies to help students develop a sense of belonging in the school and a sense of ownership over their learning. Creating that sense of belonging begins early with the ninth-grade transition program, which pairs upperclassmen with the new arrivals and offers the freshmen support and guidance during their year of adjustment.

The Forest Grove house structure also helps to establish peer-to-peer as well as student teacher connections. Students in grades 9 and 10 are divided into houses, and upperclassmen are encouraged to pursue a more specialized course of study through the school's six academies. The house structure—in which students have the same English, science, and social studies teachers—is ideal for teaming and enables the teams to plan together, address individual student needs, and implement individual interventions.

During the first semester of grade 9, each student is introduced to the "plan and profile" and begins to document experiences and academic and career learning plans for high school and beyond. Profiles are updated in the fall of each year, and learning plans are attached to each student's class records for forecasting in the spring. Learning plans are completed within an advisory structure that keeps students in the same group throughout their Forest Grove careers. Every student in the school meets with his or her adviser to review and discuss academic information, transcripts, course selection issues, school and class issues, and various school reports.

In addition to completing and monitoring individual learning plans, advisers meet with their advisory group biweekly to address grade-level issues and explore the advisory curriculum. In grade 9, the emphasis of the advisory curriculum is on making a successful transition to high school and understanding and coping with such issues as drugs, bullying, and harassment. In grade 10, advisories focus on driving, career awareness, and job shadowing.

Students in grade 11 throw most of their energy behind gathering information from speakers and other resources about colleges and careers. Senior year advisories help students to prepare for a new world of learning, financial responsibility, and personal financial literacy. The A/B block schedule—with 88 minutes in a block—offers the flexibility to use teaming, common planning time, advisories, parent conferences, and other strategies to personalize learning.

Curriculum, Instruction, and Assessment

Because promotion standards require that all eighth-grade students meet standards to attend high school, students are focusing on high school achievement before they even enter ninth grade. Failure to meet the promotion standards results in placement in a six-week summer program.

Once students enter Forest Grove, there is a similar emphasis on individual student success. One way that Forest Grove fosters achievement is by placing its best teachers with struggling students. A challenging curriculum for all students is also promoted by the Forest Grove policy of open access to AP classes. With open access and the addition of two new AP classes (for a total of 23) during the 2010–11 school year, the number of seats filled in AP courses rose from 180 to more than 500. AP participation rates among low-income students increased from 8% to 21%, and Hispanic student participation nearly doubled—from 8% to 14%—all in the course of just one year. To give more students access and to accommodate the varying paces of students, Forest Grove offers some AP classes over the entire year, instead of a semester. Another opportunity for students to engage in challenging course work is through dual enrollment programs at Portland Community College and Pacific University. This option allowed 208 students to earn 1,459 credits during the 2009–10 school year.

The school's emphasis on opportunity and high achievement for all students garnered high praise from the Oregon State superintendent of schools, Susan Castillo. "Forest Grove High School is proving daily that all children can achieve amazing things—regardless of their economic or social status," said Castillo. "I am especially impressed with their collaborative leadership, deep connection with community, intense focus on testing and accountability, and the belief that every student can achieve great things—no matter what."

Because common standards and expectations are promulgated and agreed upon through the collaborative exchanges of faculty members, the curriculum is consistent across the school, and all students are exposed to the same information and learning opportunities regardless of who their teacher is. The school implemented a schoolwide policy two years ago that requires students to demonstrate their knowledge and skills on all of the identified essential standards for a course to receive credit for it. This system is designed to eliminate grade inflation and gives students multiple opportunities to demonstrate proficiency, which takes into account the fact that all students don't learn at the same rate. Improvements have already been noted on the ACT test, which is administered free of charge to all juniors. Performance grew from the average score of 18 to 20.5 in one year, with 397 students taking the exam last year.

Assessment is an ongoing activity at Forest Grove. Teachers have regular access to the data-management computer system, and they use the data to tailor instructional strategies and investigate new options. For those students who have difficulty on state assessments and do not meet state math or reading standards, 9th- and 10th-grade reading and math workshops—some of which are taught by AP teachers—are required. Students who are placed in the workshops must forego an elective class. The workshop programs use an integrated approach and effectively double the time available for students to master areas of weakness while they continue with traditional math and English course work.

In two of the math workshop classrooms, students work independently and at their individual rate of mastery using Plato software. In those classrooms, teacher-generated mini-lessons are also used to enrich instruction and address state math standards. In a third math workshop classroom, called the "finishing room," students who are very close to mastering standards engage in a number of whole-class learning activities to address higher levels of math. The reading workshop primarily uses the Accelerated Reader Program and supplements the sustained silent reading activity with journal keeping, lessons, and read-aloud activities.

Assessment takes a turn during the senior year when students spend time researching and writing their senior projects. This culminating activity is finally complete when each student makes an oral presentation to a panel of judges. On this stage, students have a window of opportunity to demonstrate many of the writing, critical thinking, and presentation skills they have gained during their four years at Forest Grove.

One Student at a Time

As a result of these and other school improvement efforts, students report that they feel connected and that they belong at Forest Grove at an overwhelming rate. Data support that finding: the drop-out rate declined from a high of 7.7% in 2002 to 2.0% in 2009. Academic performance has increased dramatically, with 80% of the students meeting or exceeding the state math assessment and reading assessment for last year, scores that are up from 37% and 49% respectively nine years ago. It's noteworthy that the state of Oregon recently moved the state assessment from 10th grade to 11th grade starting in 2010–11. As a result of Forest Grove's continued efforts of double-blocking workshop support classes along with traditional math and English classes for its juniors, as of February 2011, 86% of the school's juniors had passed the state assessments in reading and math—well on the way to more than 90% meeting or exceeding the state assessments by year's end. The school also recently received word that it had received the 2011 Continuing Success Award, the only school in the state to receive the state recognition on five separate occasions.

O'Neill cited the school's college-going rate as an example of further progress. "Nine years ago we sent approximately 40% of our high school graduates on to a two- or four-year college or university. In the class of 2010, 68% of students went on to a two- or four-year college or university. For the first time, our Hispanic student population surpassed our Caucasian student population in the college-going rate with 70% of our Hispanic students attending compared [with] 68% of our Caucasian students."

Clearly, Forest Grove staff members understand that a good high school opens a world of opportunity for all students, and they are committed to providing the necessary knowledge, skills, and experiences to meet future vocational and academic challenges. Forest Grove is a testament to the fact that improvement can be sustained even during high-level leadership transitions if a culture of high expectations has been created.

Tying It All Together

The quick-fix mentality of school improvement must go by the wayside. There is nothing quick or easy about transforming schools—if there were, it would have been accomplished long ago. The task at hand is to improve student performance by making learning personal for each student, a feat that can only be accomplished through a culture shift within schools and communities. The *Breaking Ranks* Framework has been described in some detail in this book as a four-step progression:

1. Collaboratively determine whether your school serves each student equally well
2. Investigate practices proven to personalize the learning experience for students
3. Engage in a defined process to bring the necessary changes to fruition, to incorporate them into your culture, and to make them sustainable
4. Ensure that you and your team have the right skills, behaviors, attitudes, and dispositions to create a culture conducive to making the necessary changes.

Each of these four steps could, in and of itself, be the subject of an entire book or multiple books. In fact, NASSP has developed many complementary and supplementary materials and resources for each. Discussing the breadth of what schools are all about and helping leaders improve upon the myriad components in a comprehensive and systematic way is difficult to cover in anything less than encyclopedic volumes. Instead, we have provided school leaders with a framework to guide discussion and improvement.

Although extensive recommendations and strategies are offered in this book, the most important piece to remember is that school culture is the variable that will cause your initiatives to succeed or fail. Using the process circle, a defined and systematic approach, will help you build culture while ensuring that your school is ready for the comprehensive improvement that is described in the recommendations. Students, teachers, administrators, and others can and must provide the leadership for this culture shift.

"Leadership is the capacity to translate vision into reality," noted Bennis (2008). To accomplish that translation, perhaps the most important skill the school principal and other leaders can bring to the table is that of understanding and managing the complex changes that must occur if schools are to improve. What is required is "deep change (that) alters the system in fundamental ways, offering a dramatic shift in direction and requiring new ways of thinking and acting"—what Marzano, Waters, and McNulty

> Sustainability is very much a matter of changes in culture: powerful strategies that enable people to question and alter certain values and beliefs as they create new forms of learning within and between schools, and across levels of the system.
>
> (Fullan, 2004, p. 60)

(2005) refer to as "second-order" change. What most schools instead produce is "first-order" change: "incremental change (that) fine-tunes the system through a series of small steps that do not depart radically from the past" (p. 66).

The *Breaking Ranks* Framework is about second-order change. It is about taking all of the programs, practices, and initiatives that provide incremental change and inserting them into a larger framework for improvement that alters the system in fundamental ways. That said, not all programs, practices, and initiatives in place in a school may be appropriate; therefore, everything must be reexamined and reviewed as part of the culture shift and second-order change process. Use the *Breaking Ranks* Framework as your organizer for this effort.

By focusing on the process as well as the reform initiatives, we hope to upend the oft-expressed sentiment coined by Irene Peter, "Just because everything is different doesn't mean anything has changed." For too long educators have looked for a silver bullet that will solve schools' problems. A good idea is read or heard at a conference, brought back to the school, and implemented immediately. In the urgency to solve the problem, changes are made without thought to the big picture. As a consequence, things may look different, but nothing of significance has really changed. School leaders who wish to move beyond that quick-fix mentality must do two things: First, they must recognize the critical role that a school's belief system plays in the sustainability of school improvement efforts. Second, they must carefully examine the process they are employing to implement the change.

The Venn diagram used throughout the book illustrates the need for a well-defined framework and process for improvement. Venn diagrams are intended to make complex relationships between items easy to understand, but that certainly does not mean that they are easy to achieve. The task ahead truly is challenging. Alter one element related to creating advisories or some other initiative designed to personalize learning, for example, and suddenly instructional time, teacher contracts, and the bus schedule are also affected. And questions arise about how the time will be used to learn more about the student so that a personal plan for that student to succeed academically, socially, and emotionally can be created. Or how the student's parents or guardians will be included in the plan. And so on.

Few enterprises are more complex than schools. The Venn diagram and the "why," "what," "how," and "who" questions contained in this book can help stakeholders understand that complexity, but not be overwhelmed by it. Without delving into why your school needs to improve, it is not likely that the necessary culture shift will ever take place. Without a philosophical, structural, and process-oriented framework that advocates for improved performance for each student, only minimal and halting improvement can occur. The *Breaking Ranks* Framework can help foster a culture that puts each student at the center of your efforts.

As the original *Breaking Ranks* made clear, many people have had their say about how to improve schools—governors, legislators, policymakers, scholars from higher education, editorial writers, and others—now it is time for those who are responsible for the day-to-day operations of schools to take the lead. The *Breaking Ranks* Framework provides you with the resources to make that happen.

Appendices

This tool has been adapted for inclusion in *Breaking Ranks: The Comprehensive Framework for School Improvement*.

Step 1: Write a "best guess response" to each of the questions below.

Step 2: After you write each response, rate your degree of satisfaction with the response using the 5-point scale below.

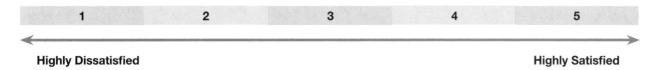

| 1 | 2 | 3 | 4 | 5 |

Highly Dissatisfied   **Highly Satisfied**

Question ˙	Write your best response	Degree of Satisfaction
How often do instructional teams, grade-level teams, and departments in your school regularly use data to plan, differentiate and deliver developmentally appropriate instruction?		
How much time is scheduled and used each week for teachers to collaborate on planning instruction, reviewing student work, aligning instructional units with standards, and encouraging interdisciplinary learning?		
How often do school administrators attend grade level, team and/or department planning meetings?		
What percentage of the schools' teachers would say they have received adequate professional development and the time to collaboratively and regularly assess student data and plan for instruction?		
What percentage of instruction at each grade level relies on active inquiry, hands-on, and project-based learning?		
What percentage of the curriculum and instruction links to real-life applications and helps students connect their education to their future?		

Question	Write your best response	Degree of Satisfaction
What percentage of each student's classroom assessment is authentic (e.g. portfolio reviews, student-led presentations, student projects) and provides multiple opportunities to demonstrate mastery?		
How frequently do classroom lessons include skills in critical thinking, problem solving, decision making, or communicating?		
What percentage of students is involved in ongoing programs that develop skills in organization, study skills, conflict resolution, self-awareness, personal safety, and stress management?		
How well does the percentage of students achieving at a proficient or higher level of performance reflect the school's demographics?		
What programs and interventions are in place to help struggling students? What percentage of struggling students takes advantage of the additional help?		
What percentage of your students must take remedial courses or other recovery programs as they transition to middle school, high school, or college?		
What percentage of teachers, students, and parents would say that transition into and out of your school is effective and appropriate?		
What percentage of students says they are well-known by at least one adult in the school who knows their aspirations, strengths, and weaknesses and who helps them be successful?		
What opportunities are students given to provide input and feedback into the academic and social activities? What percentage of students takes advantage of these opportunities?		
How often do staff members interact with parents— especially those who are hard to reach or are non-English speakers?		
What programs or services does the school provide that promote age-appropriate awareness and/or preparation for college and the work force? What percentage of students takes advantage of these opportunities?		
To what extent is the enrollment in courses or programs for gifted and talented, special education, and English language learners reflective of the school's demographics?		

Question	Write your best response	Degree of Satisfaction
How do your student recognition practices reflect how the school values diversity, service, and academic achievement? How well does the percentage of students receiving recognition reflect the demographics of the student body?		
How well do your discipline statistics reflect the demographics of the student body?		

Note: This instrument is not an exhaustive list of the questions that one can ask to gauge effectiveness of a school; however, it will begin the conversation.

Step 3: For each rating of 3 or below, consider what actions must be taken to make your satisfaction rating for that item a 5.

Step 4: Consider the implications for you and your colleagues if you believe your answers are accurate indicators of how well your school serves the needs of each student.

APPENDIX 2: MIDDLE LEVEL MATRIX

	Breaking Ranks Recommendations	*This We Believe: Keys to Educating Young Adolescents* Characteristics	*The National Forum to Accelerate Middle-Grades Reform* Schools-to-Watch Criteria
High expectations supported by engaging instruction and balanced assessments	▪ The school's instructional practices and organizational policies demonstrate its belief that each student—with work, effort, and support—can achieve at high levels. ▪ Teachers plan and deliver challenging, developmentally appropriate lessons that actively engage each student; emphasize depth over breadth; and develop skills, such as creative and critical-thinking, problem-solving, decision-making, and communication. ▪ Teachers design and use formative and summative assessments to inform instruction, advance learning, accommodate individual learning needs, and monitor student progress. ▪ The school creates a safe, caring environment characterized by interactions between adults and students that convey high expectations, support, and mutual respect.	▪ Curriculum is challenging, integrative, exploratory and relevant ▪ Educators use multiple learning and teaching approaches. ▪ Students and teachers are engaged in purposeful, active learning. ▪ Varied and ongoing assessments advance learning as well as measure it.	▪ All students are expected to meet high academic standards. ▪ The curriculum emphasizes deep understanding of important concepts and the development of essential skills. ▪ Teachers use an interdisciplinary approach to reinforce important concepts, skills, and address real-world problems.
Organizational structures promote academic growth & personal development	▪ The school establishes structures and practices to banish anonymity and individualize the learning experience for each student. ▪ The school reduces the number of students each teacher is responsible for teaching to provide each student with individualized high-quality instruction, feedback, and support. ▪ The school implements scheduling and student grouping practices that are flexible, meet each student's needs, and ensure successful academic growth and personal development. ▪ The school offers alternatives to tracking and ability grouping while maintaining the flexibility to appropriately support and challenge each student. ▪ The school fosters collaboration to improve student performance through such structures as teacher teams and regularly scheduled common planning time. ▪ The school ensures a smooth academic and social transition for each student from grade to grade and school to school.	▪ Organizational structures foster purposeful learning and meaningful relationships. ▪ Students and teachers are engaged in purposeful, active learning. ▪ Every student's academic and personal development is guided by an adult advocate. ▪ Educators use multiple learning and teaching approaches.	▪ Teachers know what each student has learned and still needs to learn. ▪ The adults in the school are provided time and frequent opportunities to enhance student achievement by working with colleagues to deepen their knowledge and to improve their standards-based practice.

Curriculum is challenging, aligned and relevant	■ The school identifies essential learnings and the standards for mastery in all subjects ■ The school connects its curriculum to real-life applications and extends learning opportunities beyond its campus. ■ The school supports and extends academic learning and personal development for each student through such structures as service learning, community service, and student activities. ■ Teachers plan and deliver challenging, developmentally appropriate lessons that actively engage each student; emphasize depth over breadth; and develop skills, such as creative and critical-thinking, problem-solving, decision-making, and communication. ■ Teachers design and use formative and summative assessments to inform instruction, advance learning, accommodate individual learning needs, and monitor student progress.	■ Curriculum is challenging, integrative, exploratory, and relevant. ■ Varied and ongoing assessments advance learning as well as measure it. ■ Organizational structures foster purposeful learning and meaningful relationships. ■ Educators use multiple learning and teaching approaches.	■ Curriculum, instruction, assessment, and appropriate academic interventions are aligned with high standards. ■ The curriculum is both socially significant and relevant to the personal and career interests of young adolescents. ■ The staff creates a personalized environment that supports each student's intellectual, ethical, social, and physical development.
Safe, healthy, personalized environment	■ The school collaboratively develops and reviews with each student a personal plan for progress that promotes ownership of the student's learning goals and provides strategies for achieving high standards. ■ The school establishes structures and practices to banish anonymity and individualize the learning experience for each student. ■ The school creates a safe, caring environment characterized by interactions between adults and students that convey high expectations, support, and mutual respect. ■ The school coordinates with community agencies in the delivery of social, physical, and mental health services to meet the needs of students and their families. ■ The school values diversity and fosters an array of viewpoints, perspectives, and experiences.	■ Every student's academic and personal development is guided by an adult advocate. ■ Comprehensive guidance and support services meet the needs of young adolescents ■ The school environment is inviting, safe, inclusive, and supportive of all. ■ School-wide programs, policies, and curricula promote health and wellness.	■ The school provides access to comprehensive services to foster healthy physical, social, emotional, and intellectual development ■ The school provides age-appropriate, co-curricular activities to foster social skills and character, and to develop interests beyond the classroom environment. ■ The school community knows every student well. ■ The schools rules are clear, fair, and consistently applied.

	Breaking Ranks Recommendations	This We Believe: Keys to Educating Young Adolescents Characteristics	The National Forum to Accelerate Middle-Grades Reform Schools-to-Watch Criteria
Multiple approaches to teaching and learning	■ Teachers plan and deliver challenging, developmentally appropriate lessons that actively engage each student; emphasize depth over breadth; and develop skills, such as creative and critical-thinking, problem-solving, decision-making, and communication. ■ Teachers design and use formative and summative assessments to inform instruction, advance learning, accommodate individual learning needs, and monitor student progress. ■ Teachers promote active engagement of each student in his or her own learning through coaching and facilitating. ■ The staff and students use current technology to improve instruction, enhance individualized learning, and facilitate management and operations.	■ Educators use multiple learning and teaching approaches. ■ Students and teachers are engaged in purposeful, active learning. ■ Varied and ongoing assessments advance learning as well as measure it. ■ Leaders are committed to and knowledgeable about this age group, educational research, and best practices.	■ Instructional strategies include a variety of challenging and engaging activities that are clearly related to the grade-level standards, concepts, and skills being taught. ■ Teachers use a variety of methods to assess and monitor the progress of student learning. ■ Teachers foster curiosity, creativity and the development of social skills in a structured and supportive environment. ■ Students are provided multiple opportunities to explore a rich variety of topics and interests in order to develop their identity, learn about their strengths, discover and demonstrate their own competence, and plan for their future. ■ Students are provided the opportunity to use many and varied approaches to achieve and demonstrate competence and mastery of standards.
Prepared, knowledgeable teachers & principals	■ Each educator possesses pedagogical expertise, a broad academic foundation, in-depth content knowledge in the subjects taught, and an understanding of the developmental needs of his or her students ■ The school fosters collaboration to improve student performance through structures, such as teacher teams and regularly scheduled common planning time.	■ Educators value young adolescents and are prepared to teach them. ■ Leaders are committed to and knowledgeable about this age group, educational research, and best practices. ■ Leaders demonstrate courage and collaboration. ■ Organizational structures foster purposeful learning and meaningful relationships. ■ Varied and ongoing assessments advance learning as well as measure it.	■ The faculty and master schedule provide students time to meet rigorous academic standards. ■ The adults in the school are provided time and frequent opportunities to enhance student achievement by working with colleagues to deepen their knowledge and to improve their standards-based practice. ■ Teachers continually adapt curriculum, instruction, assessment, and scheduling to meet their students' diverse and changing needs.

Democratic, Collaborative Leadership	<ul><li>The principal leads in developing, articulating and committing to a shared vision and mission focused on student success.</li><li>The school provides meaningful decision-making roles for staff, students, and parents.</li><li>All members of the school community actively collaborate to develop and implement the agreed-upon learning goals and improvement plan.</li><li>Teachers and teacher teams provide leadership essential to student success</li><li>The school develops partnerships with individuals, organizations, community agencies, and businesses to support its mission.</li><li>The school, in addition to its continuous monitoring of progress and yearly reporting, will convene a broad-based panel to conduct an in-depth assessment and present their findings to the public at least once every three years.</li><li>The school and students' families are partners in fostering the academic, intellectual, social, and emotional success of each student.</li></ul>	<ul><li>Leaders demonstrate courage and collaboration.</li><li>A shared vision that is developed by all stakeholders guides every decision.</li><li>The school actively involves families in the education of their children.</li><li>The school includes community and business groups as partners.</li></ul>	<ul><li>All students have opportunities for voice – posing questions, reflecting on experiences, and participating in decisions and leadership activities.</li><li>The school staff members develop alliances with families to enhance and support the well-being of the children.</li><li>Staff members provide all students with opportunities to develop citizenship skills, to use the community as a classroom and to engage the community in providing resources and support.</li><li>The faculty welcomes and encourages the active participation of all its families and makes sure that all its families are an integral part of the school.</li></ul>
Equity and access for every student	<ul><li>The school values diversity and fosters an array of viewpoints, perspectives, and experiences.</li><li>The school advocates and models a set of core values that are essential in a democratic and civil society.</li><li>The school offers alternatives to tracking and ability grouping while maintaining the flexibility to appropriately support and challenge each student.</li></ul>	<ul><li>The school environment is inviting, safe, inclusive, and supportive of all.</li><li>Curriculum is challenging, integrative, exploratory and relevant</li><li>Organizational structures foster purposeful learning and meaningful relationships.</li></ul>	<ul><li>To the fullest extent possible, all students, including English learners, students with disabilities, gifted and honors students, participate in heterogeneous classes with high academic and behavioral expectations.</li><li>All students have ongoing opportunities to learn about and appreciate their own and others' cultures.</li><li>The school's reward system is designed to value diversity, civility, service, and democratic citizenship.</li><li>Staff members understand and support the family backgrounds and values of its students.</li></ul>

	Breaking Ranks in the Middle Recommendations	This We Believe: Keys to Educating Young Adolescents Characteristics	The National Forum to Accelerate Middle-Grades Reform Schools-to-Watch Criteria
Committed to professional development	■ All members of the school community actively collaborate to develop and implement the agreed-upon learning goals and improvement plan. ■ Each staff member develops a personal learning plan (PLP) aligned with the school improvement plan. ■ The school develops partnerships with postsecondary institutions to enhance learning for students and adults. ■ The school fosters collaboration to improve student performance through such structures as teacher teams and regularly scheduled common planning time.	■ Ongoing professional development reflects best educational practices. ■ A shared vision that is developed by all stakeholders guides every decision. ■ Educators value young adolescents and are prepared to teach them. ■ Leaders are committed to and knowledgeable about this age group, educational research, and best practices. ■ Educators use multiple learning and teaching approaches. ■ School-wide programs, policies, and curricula promote health and wellness.	■ The adults in the school are provided time and frequent opportunities to enhance student achievement by working with colleagues to deepen their knowledge and to improve their standards-based practice.

APPENDIX 3
CURRICULUM, INSTRUCTION, AND ASSESSMENT:
RIGOR AND RELEVANCE

The old adage of learning best by experience is really true. Research confirms that more learning occurs when students are immersed in a rich, stimulating environment. Learning that involves a physical component, such as writing or design and construction, results in greater brain activity than simply listening or viewing. To be effective, education must create these types of stimulating learning experiences.

Application also improves learning. William Glasser's research findings in communication and learning reinforces what we all know innately—learners retain information better when they actually use or apply it. Students retain 75 percent or more of what they experience through application. New information presented only through lecture results in a retention rate of 5 percent. Reading can increase that rate to 10 percent. Adding audiovisual material results in a 20 percent retention rate.

Figure A3.1
Learning Activity Retention

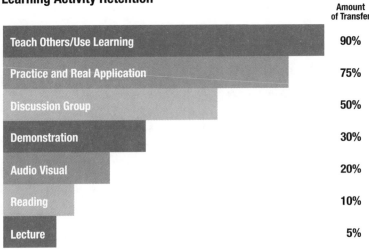

	Amount of Transfer
Teach Others/Use Learning	90%
Practice and Real Application	75%
Discussion Group	50%
Demonstration	30%
Audio Visual	20%
Reading	10%
Lecture	5%

Unfortunately, students in U.S. classrooms have limited exposure to application. Other nations equate application with high-level learning and frequently incorporate real-world problems into instruction. Stevenson and Stigler point to analysis of classroom instruction that reveal that only 16 percent of instruction in a sample of U.S. classrooms could be characterized as application. In contrast, instruction in Taiwan and Japan was 62 percent and 82 percent application, respectively. Citing a large body of research, ICLE asserts the following:

- Knowledge is best acquired when taught in context
- Increased achievement results from focusing on students' interests and aptitudes
- Meta-cognition is essential for continued learning
- High expectations correlate with achievement

ICLE's Rigor/Relevance Framework®

The Rigor/Relevance Framework is based on two dimensions of higher standards and student achievement:

- A continuum of knowledge that describes the increasingly complex ways in which learners think (Bloom's Knowledge Taxonomy).
- An action continuum, known as the Application Model.

The Knowledge Taxonomy is based on the six levels of Bloom's Taxonomy: (1) awareness/knowledge, (2) comprehension, (3) application, (4) analysis, (5) synthesis, and (6) evaluation. The low end of this continuum involves acquiring knowledge and being able to recall or locate that knowledge in a simple manner. The high end of the Knowledge Taxonomy labels more complex ways in which individuals use knowledge. At this level knowledge is fully integrated into one's mind, and individuals can do much more than locate information. They can take several pieces of knowledge and combine them in both logical and creative ways. Assimilation of knowledge is a good way to describe this high level of the thinking continuum. Assimilation is often referred to as a higher-order thinking skills; at this level, the student can solve multi-step problems and create unique work and solutions. A look at how these various levels can be applied in classroom activities related to basic nutrition may help the reader visualize.

Figure A3.2

Basic Nutrition	
Level	**Performance**
Level 1 – Knowledge/Awareness	Label foods by nutritional groups
Level 2 – Comprehension	Explain nutritional value of individual foods
Level 3 – Application	Make use of nutrition guidelines in planning meals
Level 4 – Analysis	Examine success in achieving nutrition goals
Level 5 – Synthesis	Develop personal nutrition goals
Level 6 – Evaluation	Appraise results of personal eating habits over time

The second continuum, the Application Model, is one of action. The five levels of this continuum describe putting knowledge to use:

- knowledge in one discipline
- apply in discipline
- apply across disciplines
- apply to real-world predictable situations
- apply to real-world unpredictable situations.

While the low end of the continuum is knowledge acquired for its own sake, the high end signifies action—use of that knowledge to solve complex real-world problems and to create projects, designs, and other works for use in real-world situations.

Figure A3.3

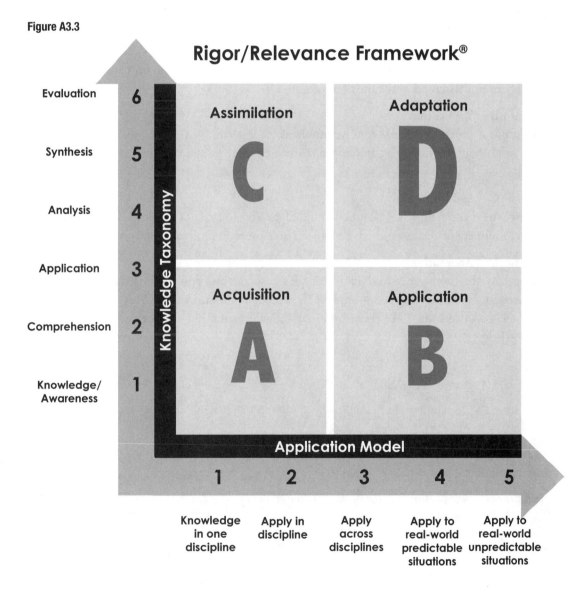

The Rigor/Relevance Framework has four quadrants.

Quadrant A represents simple recall and basic understanding of knowledge for its own sake. Quadrant C represents more complex thinking but still knowledge for its own sake. Examples of Quadrant A knowledge are knowing that the world is round and that Shakespeare wrote *Hamlet*.

Quadrant C embraces higher levels of knowledge, such as knowing how the U.S. political system works and analyzing the benefits and challenges of the cultural diversity of this nation versus other nations.

Quadrants B and D represent action or high degrees of application. Quadrant B would include knowing how to use math skills to make purchases and count change. The ability to access information in wide-area network systems and the ability to gather knowledge from a variety of sources to solve a complex problem in the workplace are types of Quadrant D knowledge.

Each of these four quadrants can also be labeled with a term that characterizes the learning or student performance.

Quadrant A   Acquisition

Students gather and store bits of knowledge and information. Students are primarily expected to remember or understand this acquired knowledge.

Quadrant B   Application

Students use acquired knowledge to solve problems, design solutions, and complete work. The highest level of application is to apply appropriate knowledge to new and unpredictable situations.

Quadrant C   Assimilation

Students extend and refine their acquired knowledge to be able to use that knowledge automatically and routinely to analyze and solve problems and create unique solutions.

Quadrant D   Adaptation

Students have the competence to think in complex ways and also apply knowledge and skills they have acquired. Even when confronted with perplexing unknowns, students are able to use extensive knowledge and skill to create solutions and take action that further develops their skills and knowledge.

Quadrant A—Acquisition: Experiences focus on recall or discovery of basic knowledge.

Quadrant B—Application: Activities provide definite opportunities for students to apply knowledge, typically to real-world problem.

Quadrant C—Assimilation: Activities are often complex and require students to often come up with solutions that lead to deeper understanding of concepts and knowledge.

Quadrant D—Adaptation: Learning experiences are high in rigor and relevance and require unique solutions to unpredictable problems.

But how can a teacher or educational leader evaluate where a specific lesson, task, application, assessment or activity falls within this continuum. ICLE developed the Knowledge Taxonomy Verb List and Application Model Decision Tree [insert below] to help analyze the material and describe or revise desired performance objectives. The Verb List mirrors the knowledge levels. The Decision Tree focuses on the three characteristics that distinguish levels of the Application Model: application, real world, and unpredictability.

Figure A3.4

KNOWLEDGE TAXONOMY VERB LIST

1 KNOWLEDGE

arrange	match
check	name
choose	point to
find	recall
group	recite
identify	repeat
label	say
list	select
locate	write

2 COMPREHENSION

advance	interpret
calculate	outline
change	project
contemplate	propose
convert	reword
define	submit
explain	transform
extrapolate	translate
infer	vary

3 APPLICATION

adopt	manipulate
capitalize on	mobilize
consume	operate
devote	put to use
employ	relate
exercise	solve
handle	start
maintain	take up
make use of	utilize

4 ANALYSIS

assay	include
audit	inspect
break down	look at
canvass	scrutinize
check out	sift
deduce	study
dissect	survey
divide	test for
examine	uncover

5 SYNTHESIS

blend	develop
build	evolve
cause	form
combine	generate
compile	make up
compose	originate
conceive	produce
construct	reorder
create	structure

6 EVALUATION

accept	grade
appraise	judge
arbitrate	prioritize
assess	rank
award	rate
classify	reject
criticize	rule on
decide	settle
determine	weigh

Application Model Decision Tree

Directions: Select a task, application, or activity and then answer the following questions. See next page for clarification of the questions.

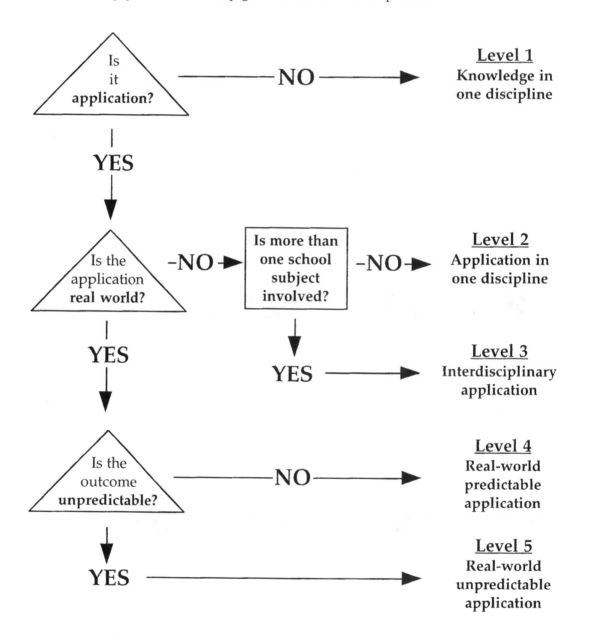

Application Model Decision Tree

Directions: Use the following statements to clarify where a task, application, or assessment belongs on the Application Model.

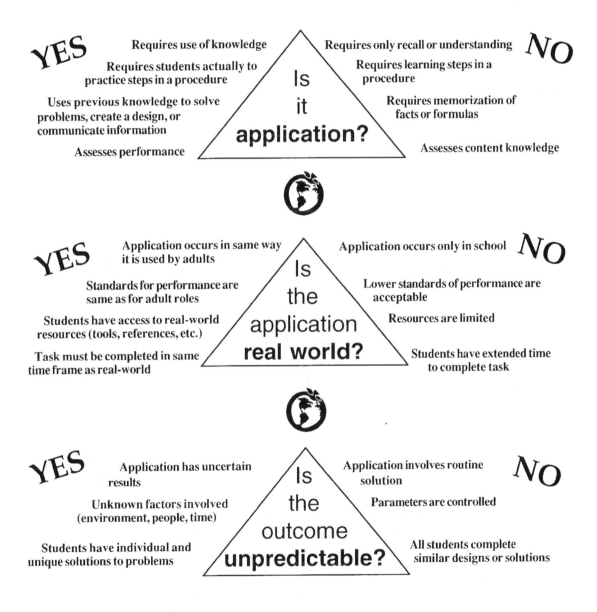

YES

Requires use of knowledge

Requires students actually to practice steps in a procedure

Uses previous knowledge to solve problems, create a design, or communicate information

Assesses performance

Is it application?

NO

Requires only recall or understanding

Requires learning steps in a procedure

Requires memorization of facts or formulas

Assesses content knowledge

YES

Application occurs in same way it is used by adults

Standards for performance are same as for adult roles

Students have access to real-world resources (tools, references, etc.)

Task must be completed in same time frame as real-world

Is the application real world?

NO

Application occurs only in school

Lower standards of performance are acceptable

Resources are limited

Students have extended time to complete task

YES

Application has uncertain results

Unknown factors involved (environment, people, time)

Students have individual and unique solutions to problems

Is the outcome unpredictable?

NO

Application involves routine solution

Parameters are controlled

All students complete similar designs or solutions

Why is this Useful?

One of the principles of effective learning is congruence among curriculum, instruction, and assessment. Make sure that the levels of rigor and relevance are consistent throughout a lesson. For example, if a teacher has lofty curriculum objectives in Quadrant D—high rigor/high relevance but develops instruction and assessments in Quadrant A—low rigor/low relevance, students would be unlikely to achieve those high expectations. Similarly, if a teacher creates high-rigor instructional activities but uses a low-rigor assessment, the test would not be an accurate indication of what students learned.

Use the Application Model Decision Tree to draft, examine and modify curriculum objectives, instructional activities or assessments to get them to the desired level.

One of the ways to think about the Rigor/Relevance Framework in day-to-day instruction is in terms of the roles that teachers and students take.

Figure A3.6

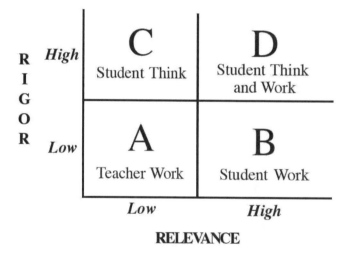

When instruction and expected student learning is in Quadrant A, the focus is on "teacher work." Teachers expend energy to create and assess learning activities—providing information, creating worksheets, and grading student work. The student is often the passive learner.

When the student expectation moves to Quadrant B, the emphasis is on the student doing real-world work. This student work is often more complicated than Quadrant A work and requires more time. Learning in Quadrant B is best described as "student work" because students are doing extensive real-world tasks.

When the learning is placed in Quadrant C, it is best described as "student think." In this Quadrant, students are expected to think in complex ways—to analyze, compare, create and evaluate.

The term that best describes Quadrant D activities is "student think and work." Learning Quadrant D is more demanding. Roles shift from the teacher-centered instruction in Quadrant A to student-centered instruction in Quadrants B, C, and D.

What it Looks Like in Practice

The charts on the following pages provide examples at the elementary, middle level and high school to help teachers and school leaders distinguish the types of activities that would be called for in the various quadrants.

Figure A3.7

Learning Experiences in the Rigor/Relevance Framework

Mathematics	Elementary Examples

Quadrant **C** Assimilation

6

- Predict and analyze patterns of sides of three-dimensional boxes.
- Use pattern blocks to construct desired shapes.

5
- Identify next numbers in a sequence.
- Find values in number sentences when represented by unknowns.
- Round off numbers and estimate answers.
- Use a balance to predict and determine equivalent value.

4
- Create math word problems for younger students.

Quadrant **D** Adaptation

- Develop formula for determining a large quantity without counting, such as beans in a jar.
- Calculate change of values to double or halve a recipe.
- Discover similar characteristics of different geometric solids.
- Collect data on an event and compare to expected results (e.g., the number of faulty parts manufactured).
- Evaluate situations when estimates are acceptable and unacceptable.
- Create a measurement scale (e.g., hand span, book, length of string) and measure objects in classroom.

3 -

Quadrant **A** Acquisition

- Explore likenesses and differences of objects (color, shape, size).

2
- Sort and classify objects, such as buttons, blocks, bottle tops.
- Use color counters to solve simple computational problems
- Divide objects to illustrate whole, half, third, quarter.

1
- Construct shapes and patterns with craft sticks.
- Memorize multiplication tables.
- Find the lines of symmetry in letters of the alphabet and numerals.
- Use pegboards to discover multiplied values.

Quadrant **B** Application

- Divide quantities of objects into equal groups.
- Calculate the area of objects.
- Make a graph comparing characteristics of two groups.
- Find patterns outdoors and indoors.
- Collect temperatures at different times of day for several days and make a graph to display recorded data.
- Use rulers to measure objects.
- Sort quantities to discover fractions of the whole.

1   2   3   4   5

Learning Experiences in the Rigor/Relevance Framework

| English Language Arts |
| Middle Level Examples |

6

Quadrant C Assimilation

- Play word games to identify specific language usage, such as figurative language.
- Research the history of words and phrases.

5

- Keep a journal of reflection on literature.
- Write a creative story, such as surviving in the wilderness.
- Create analogies to explain an idea.
- Analyze commercials for fact and opinion.
- Analyze a character in a novel.

4

- Create a new character in mythology.

Quadrant D Adaptation

- Create a Bill of Rights for your school or classroom.
- Write directions for assembling a product or carrying out a procedure.
- Create a rubric for evaluating writing assignments.
- Research and debate a controversial issue.
- Write a folk tale based on contemporary life.
- Analyze and rewrite political cartoons.

3 -

Quadrant A Acquisition

2

- View movies that depict human emotions and behaviors.
- Label parts of speech in sentences.
- Look up the definition of the "word of the day."
- Use library reference tools.

1

- Give oral directions.
- Read nonfiction or historical literature.
- Locate and describe technical writing.

Quadrant B Application

- Conduct an interview.
- Conduct a meeting using parliamentary procedure.
- Conduct an Internet search.
- Write captions for cartoons.
- Lead a class discussion on a current event.
- Assemble a product following written directions.
- Write articles and headlines for a class newsletter.
- Act out characters in a story.

1   **2**   **3**   **4**   **5**

Learning Experiences in the Rigor/Relevance Framework

Science	High School Examples

6

5

4

3

Quadrant C Assimilation

- Solve a hypothetical science-related problem, such as helping dinosaurs to survive.
- Design experiments and collect evidence to describe the movement of light.
- Design a WebQuest on an aspect of chemistry.
- Design observations to demonstrate basic laws of physics.
- Calculate potential and kinetic energy in the movement of a roller coaster.
- Create a digital electronic counter.
- Write test questions to illustrate understanding of empirical gas laws.
- Research the discovery of a chemical element.

Quadrant D Adaptation

- Explore designs of car safety restraints using eggs in model cars.
- Design and construct a robot.
- Conduct debate on genetically modified food (GMF).
- Solve an organic chemistry case study problem in petroleum distillation.
- Select a method to build a tunnel under a real city.
- Discuss the social, ethical, and emotional consequences of genetic testing.
- Participate in an online debate on a science issue, such as acid rain or deformed frogs.
- Research and write a newspaper article on a viral disease, examining economic and societal impacts.

2

1

Quadrant A Acquisition

- Conduct laboratory experiments to observe chemical reactions.
- Apply number and computation skills in science, including scientific notation and significant figures.
- Determine latitude and longitude of geographic locations.
- Use a mnemonic system for remembering metric conversions.
- Demonstrate modulation of sound waves using computer animation.
- Conduct experiments to observe properties of acids and bases.
- Memorize elements in Periodic Table.
- Make observations about the visual effects of concave and convex lenses.

Quadrant B Application

- Map a community site by collecting data with GPS device.
- Collect and categorize organisms from a natural stream.
- Apply Laws of Gases to design gas storage containers.
- Make weather forecasts based on data.
- Solve electrical current values using Ohm's law.
- Isolate DNA from unknown plant tissues and compare to sample DNA.
- Participate in an online collaboration to collect scientific data on a global problem.

1   2   3   4   5

The ICLE Rigor/Relevance Framework provides an excellent starting point for your team to begin a thorough look at ensuring that the curriculum is rigorous and relevant, that the instruction and activities are designed to move students beyond acquisition of facts and that the assessment tools are aligned with higher order skills and knowledge. Clearly this overview can only provide a starting point for your thinking and discussions around improving student learning.

Is Instruction Engaging?

As the principal or a member of the leadership team, you are responsible for gathering and analyzing information about the instructional practices in your school and their overall effectiveness. Is it feasible to develop a schoolwide picture of student learning that can serve as the basis for faculty reflection, instructional change, and school improvement? More specifically,

- How do you collect data that will be accepted by faculty as a fair and accurate representation of student learning throughout the school?
- How do you depict those data in a simple, meaningful format for analysis?
- How do you engage all faculty members in study and reflection about the data that will lead to improved instructional practices throughout the school?
- How do you use the data to document enhanced learning experiences for all students?

Note: All material in Appendix 3 was provided by ICLE, except as noted, and reprinted with permission.

Activities: Gather and Analyze Data to Determine Priorities

Worksheet

(Note: An electronic version of this worksheet is available at www.nassp.org/brguide)

Essential Elements of Each Step	
Sources of Data and Analysis	
Collaborative Leadership	
Infrastructure Capacity	
Communication and Buy-in	
Professional Development	

APPENDIX 5
ALIGNING PROFESSIONAL DEVELOPMENT WITH SCHOOL NEEDS

Collegial coaching allows educators to experience on-the-job feedback to improve their practices.

Near the end of a recent conversation about aligned *Breaking Ranks* professional development opportunities for teachers, the principal of a large, successful high school confided that she had neither adequate funding nor time for professional development activities for herself and her leadership team. What a terrible situation! Schools will not change or improve unless the performance capacity of everyone who works in the school improves. "Everyone" includes the members of the leadership team.

NASSP staff members often ask successful leaders, "How did you get to be as good as you are?" The most frequent response to the question is best summarized as, "Just by doing the job!" Their full responses reveal such concepts as learning from one's successes and mistakes; taking risks to try different approaches until finding the best one; watching others do a job successfully; making adjustments on the basis of praise, criticism, and feedback; and receiving the support and guidance of mentors and colleagues who were willing to guide, teach, and coach.

Such growth opportunities have benefited thousands of successful leaders, so school leaders short on time and funds might consider purposefully and intentionally incorporating some of the concepts into their practice through collegial coaching. Although it takes discipline and a willingness on the part of leaders to share in one another's growth for the benefit of their students, collegial coaching with a leadership team models effective professional development behavior for teachers and others.

Trust is essential among colleagues who acknowledge that they are not perfect and are seeking to learn from experiences—their own and those of coworkers. Where collegial trust is weak or does not exist, engaging in professional growth activities together may provide a foundation for it to develop or strengthen.

The ability to listen and ask the right questions is also important to the success of collegial coaching. This strategy provides opportunities for leadership teams to engage in job-embedded professional development as a part of their daily work experiences as they enhance their performance capacity and effectiveness in meeting the real needs of the school community.

Just as having a physical exam is advisable before beginning a new diet and exercise regime, an assessment of professional skills and knowledge is recommended before engaging in meaningful professional development. The leadership team's knowledge of each of its member's capacity not only enables the team to more-effectively assign responsibilities but also provides a foundation for collaborating in shared professional growth. Some of the tools for assessing professional strengths include 360-degree assessments (www.nassp.org/BRonlinetools), the NASSP online skills assessment (www.nassp.org/lsa), input and feedback from colleagues and mentors, performance appraisal data, and other assessments of talents and characteristics. Assessment of strengths and weaknesses provides members of the team with data to inform their decisions about the areas on which they want to focus their development.

Collegial Observations and Coaching

After making decisions about what skills or knowledge to develop, team members are ready to begin coaching one another. During collegial coaching:

- One colleague asks another to observe his or her performance in a specific situation to note demonstrations of specific skills or behaviors.

- During the performance, the observer records what his or her colleague says and does.

- Following the performance, the observer analyzes the data collected and prepares to give the performer feedback. Simultaneously, the performer reflects on what he or she did well and what needs improvement.

- The observer leads a feedback conversation to discuss what happened during the performance and asks the performer to share his or her reflections. The observer then shares two or three effective behaviors that he or she saw and gives one suggestion for improving the performance. He or she supports these observations and suggestions with data collected during the performance. The observer then asks questions that prompt further reflection. Both people discuss ways that the performer can build on his or her strengths and refine less-effective behaviors. They schedule a follow-up to discuss progress and challenges.

Reflection as the Basis for Collegial Coaching

When an observation is not convenient or practical, collegial coaching can be based on the performer's reflective review of a situation or event. This approach requires that the performer review and analyze his or her own behavior and to write responses to the following prompts before talking with a collegial coach.

- Describe the basic nature of the situation and explain how or why it developed.
- What are the primary issues and concerns—yours and those of others?
- What were your objectives and strategies when you approached the situation?
- What data did you have? Need, but did not have?
- Describe the essential verbal and nonverbal behavior of the people involved in the situation, including yourself.
- What are the outcomes to date? What are your reactions to those outcomes?
- What did you do to contribute positively to the outcomes? What might you have done differently to contribute to a better outcome?
- What you have learned from the situation thus far?

The performer schedules a coaching conversation to discuss the situation. Sending a copy of the reflective review will help the coach prepare in advance for the conversation. The written review also helps keep the conversation focused.

During the coaching session, the performer provides a summary of the information that was written in response to the reflective review prompts while the coach listens and makes notes to facilitate further reflection.

Following the summary, the coach leads a discussion of what happened during the situation and uses probing questions that focus on the performer's actions. The colleagues discuss and agree on next steps that will build on the strengths that the performer demonstrated in the situation and refine less-effective behaviors. They agree on a time and place for a follow-up discussion to discuss progress and challenges.

Working Together

Working together, colleagues who make up a leadership team can use their own experiences and expertise to help one another explore ways to improve performance and effectiveness.

Too frequently, seminars, workshops, courses, and other formal learning opportunities are the only strategies that come to mind when someone mentions professional development.

A school can provide the very best laboratory for the exercise, practice, and development of school leadership if leaders seize the opportunities for trying new behaviors, reflecting on their own performance, seeking and giving collegial feedback, adjusting performance on the basis of that reflection and feedback, and adapting emerging strengths to meet new and different challenges as they arise. Engaging in a process that builds the capacity of school leaders to effectively address the real issues of the school community gives deeper meaning to efforts to align professional development with the school's desired learning outcomes, the most effective instructional strategies, and the development of learners.

Source: Reed, P. (2010). Aligning professional development with school needs. *Principal Leadership, 10*(8), p. 62–64. Copyright 2010 National Association of Secondary School Principals.

Effective Listening and Questioning

Effective Listening

- Stop talking and listen to every word. If you are talking, you are not listening!

- Avoid distractions. Give the speaker your full attention; do not try to attend to other matters, such as phone calls or paperwork, during your conversation.

- Show your attention through eye contact, head nods, and attentive posture.

- Do not interrupt the other person; give the person a chance to say what he or she has to say.

- Ask probing questions to get more clarifying information, but avoid asking embarrassing or insensitive questions.

- Empathize with the other person. Reserve judgment and try to put yourself in that person's place to better understand what he or she is saying.

- Concentrate on what the person is saying and avoid thinking ahead to what you are going to say.

- Listen for what is not said. Often what a person does not say is as important to understanding the situation as what he or she does say.

- Listen to how something is said. A person's attitudes and emotional reactions may be more important than the actual words.

- Avoid making assumptions about what a person means, intends, thinks, or feels. Listen for specific information and ask clarifying questions.

- Avoid classifying the speaker. Frequently, we label someone as one type of person ("he is a conservative") and then try to fit everything the person says or does into the context of that label. This usually means that our perceptions of what that person says or means are shaded by whether we like or dislike the attributes we associate with how we've classified him or her.

- Recognize your own biases toward the speaker, the subject, and the situation. Work to overcome the effect they may have on your ability to really listen and understand the other person.

Effective Questioning

- Elicit perceptions, feelings, and concerns:

  "How do you think you handled the situation?"

  "How do you feel about the way you've handled the situation?"

  "What do you perceive as the major issues in the situation?"

  "What major concerns do you have about the situation?"

- Express verbal and nonverbal recognition of feelings:

  Paraphrase what you heard: "So what concerns you is..." and "Let's see if I understand what you've said...."

  Maintain appropriate eye contact and be aware of facial expressions.

- Accurately reflect the point of view of another:

  "You haven't been able to...."

  "You would like to...."

  "What would you like to see happen?"

  "What could you do to create a win-win situation?"

  "What I think I heard you say is...."

- Seek and give feedback:

  "What did you do well in this situation?"

  "What would you do differently?"

  "What options have you considered?"

  "Have you thought of...?"

  "Could you say more about that?"

- Explore alternatives:

  "What might you have done instead?"

  "Since you have no control over these external variables, what adjustments might you make in the things you can control?"

  "Let's brainstorm different ways to approach this and then come back and consider the implications of each."

  "What might be the result of taking that approach?"

  "What options do you see as the most viable?"

Adapted from the *Breaking Ranks: Mentoring and Coaching* professional development program.

Broader, Bolder Approach to Education. (June 25, 2009). *School accountability: A broader, bolder approach*. Washington, DC: Report of the Accountability Committee of the Broader Bolder Approach to Education Campaign.

Cawelti, G. (1999). *Portraits of six benchmark schools diverse approaches to improving student achievement*. Alexandria, VA: Educational Research Service.

Dweck, C. S. (2006). *Mindset: The new psychology of success*. New York: NY: Random House.

Jerald, C. (2005). *Planning that matters: Helping schools engage in collaborative, strategic problem solving*. Washington, DC: The Center for Comprehensive School Reform and Improvement.

Luft, J., & Ingham, H. (1955). The Johari window, a graphic model of interpersonal awareness. *Proceedings of the Western Training Laboratory in Group Development*. Los Angeles, CA: University of California–Los Angeles.

Quellmalz, E., Shields, P. M., & Knapp, M. S. (1995). *School-based reform: Lessons from a national study. A guide for school reform teams*. Menlo Park, CA: SRI International.

Reed, P. (2010, April). Aligning professional development with school needs. *Principal Leadership, 10*(8), 62–64.

Rumberger, R. W. (2009). *What the federal government can do to improve high school performance*. Washington, DC: Center on Education Policy.

Schmoker, M. J. (2011). *Focus: Elevating the essentials to radically improve student learning*. Alexandria, VA: ASCD.

Seashore Louis, K., Leithwood, K., Wahlstrom, K. L., Anderson, S. E., Michlin, M., Mascall, B., …Moore, S. (2010). *Investigating the links to improved student learning: Final report of research to the Wallace Foundation*. Retrieved from University of Minnesota, Center for Applied Research and Educational Improvement Web site: www.cehd.umn.edu/carei/Leadership/Learning-from-Leadership_Final-Report_March-2010.pdf

Wallace Foundation. (2011). *Research findings to support effective educational policies: A guide for policymakers*. New York, NY: Author.

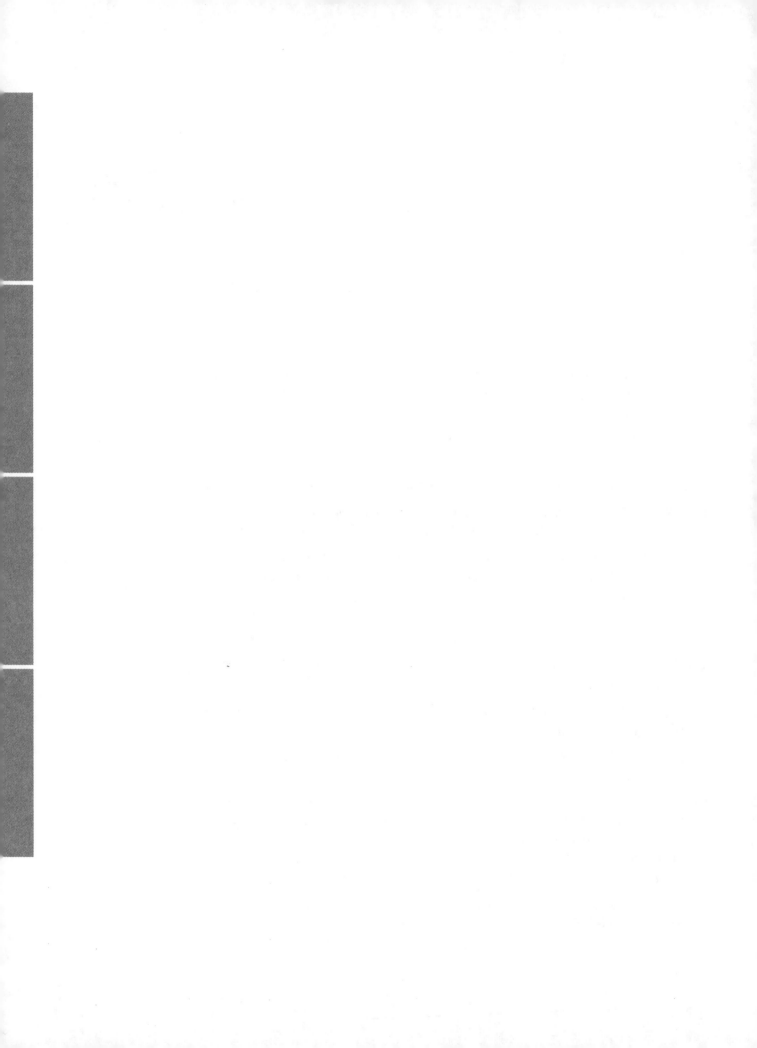

Clark, D., & Clark S. (2008). *Leadership that makes a difference: Revitalizing middle schools.* Arlington, VA: National Middle School Association.

Clarke, J. (2003). *Changing systems to personalize learning: Introduction to personalization workshops.* Providence, RI: Education Alliance at Brown University.

Fullan, M. (2005). *Leadership and sustainability: System thinkers in action.* Thousand Oaks, CA: Corwin.

Fullan, M. (2010). *All systems go: The change imperative for whole system reform.* Thousand Oaks, CA: Corwin Press & Ontario Principal's Council.

DiMartino, J., Clarke, J., & Wolk, D. (2003). *Personalized learning: Preparing high school students to create their futures.* Lanham, MD: Scarecrow Press.

Dweck, C. (2006). *Mindset: The new psychology of success.* New York, NY: Random House.

Marzano, R., Waters, R. J., Waters, T., & McNulty, B. A. (2005). *School leadership that works: From research to results.* Alexandria, VA: ASCD.

McGregor, D. (1985). *The human side of enterprise.* New York, NY: McGraw Hill.

MetaMetrics. (2011a). Common core standards and Lexile measures. Retrieved from www.lexile.com/using-lexile/lexile-measures-and-the-ccssi/

MetaMetrics. (2011b). What is a Lexile measure? Durham, NC: MetaMetrics. Retrieved from www.lexile.com/about-lexile/lexile-overview/

Mihalic, S. F., Fagan, A., Irwin, K., Ballard, D., & Elliot, D. (2004). *Blueprints for violence prevention.* Washington, DC: U.S. Department of Justice, Office of Justice Programs, Office of Juvenile Justice and Delinquency Prevention.

Mourshed, M., Chijioke, C., & Barber, M. (2010). *How the world's most improved school systems keep getting better.* Washington, DC: McKinsey&Company.

Odden, A. (2009, December 9). We know how to turn schools around—we just haven't done it. *Education Week*, 22–23.

Protheroe, N. (2011). Implementing and sustaining school improvement. *Principal's Research Review, 6*(2). Retrieved from the NASSP Web site: www.nassp.org/Content/158/prr_mar11_web.pdf

Schmoker, M. J. (2011). *Focus: Elevating the essentials to radically improve student learning.* Alexandria, VA: ASCD.

Rumberger, R. (2009). *What the federal government can do to improve high school performance* (Technical Report). Washington, DC: Center on Education Policy.

Seashore Louis, K., & Wahlstrom, K. (2011). Principals as cultural leaders. *Phi Delta Kappan, 92*(5), 52–56.